Color Your Way to
Serenity
with Mandalas

Volume 2

30 more beautiful kaleidoscope designs
to help you find your Flow

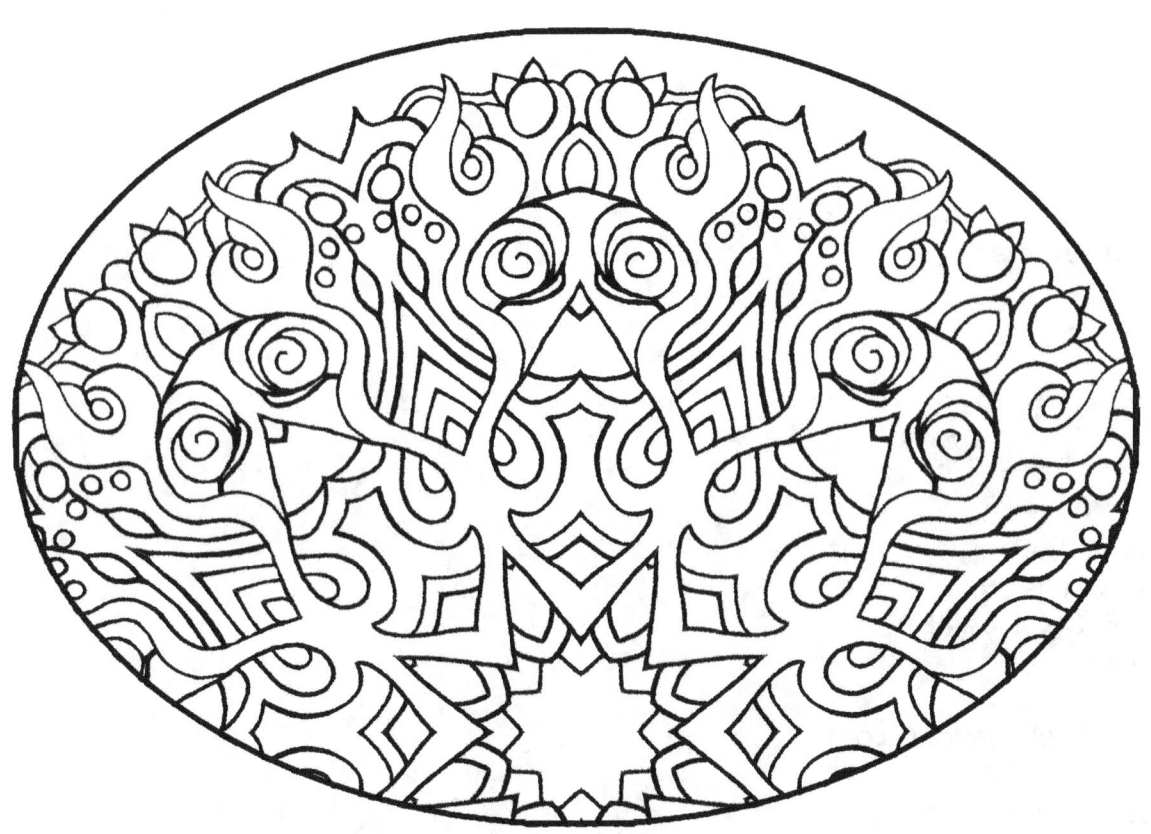

by Marian Buchanan

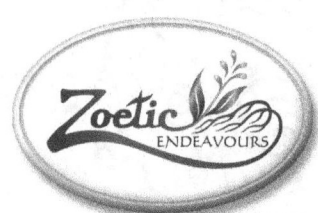

Zoetic Endeavours
P.O.Box 3049 Stn B
London ON N6A 4H9
Canada

info@zoeticendeavours.com

ZoeticEndeavours.com

www.facebook.com/ZoeticEndeavours

www.goodreads.com/MarianBuchanan

ISBN 978-0-9948837-2-8

A Word from the Artist

Did you enjoy Volume 1? Here are 30 more mandala designs, hand-drawn and then assembled into kaleidoscope patterns, created specifically with coloring in mind.

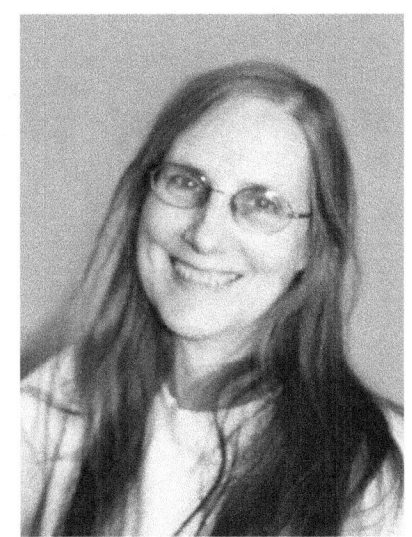

If you're already an avid colorist, you may already know what I mean when I say that coloring these mandala designs can help you "find your Flow." When you're absorbed in an artistic task — choosing your colors, applying them to the spaces between the lines, maybe even adding new lines... or coloring outside of them! — you can enter a state of serenity and ease, which is sometimes called "flow." This is why coloring books for grown-ups can be used for stress management. Of course, you can just color them for the pure pleasure of it, too!

Coloring someone else's artwork is also a way to be involved in the creativity and beauty of art even if you feel you don't know how to draw or you're not in the mood to create a picture from scratch. The coloring stage is an important contribution to a picture's overall effect. Your choices of shades and hues, whether or not to make gradients, and what medium to use, will all make a big difference in what the final artwork looks like.

At the bottom right of each design, there's a line for your name as the colorist. You can't claim copyright in the work, even once you've colored it, but you're welcome to show off your coloring efforts and creative choices in an Amazon review of the book, or on social media such as any of the many Facebook groups dedicated to adult coloring. When you do share on social media, please remember to let people know where the design comes from. It's a good way to help other colorists have a chance to color the same design, and it's also a way to show your appreciation of me as the artist. Remember: permission to share is just for your colored results, not for the blank design itself.

I'll be continuing to create more coloring books in the future, so please feel free to send me your feedback about what kinds of art you'd like to color. If you'd like to be notified when each new volume comes out, please Like my Facebook Page to get updates in your Facebook news feed, or send me an email at info@zoeticendeavours.com to request membership in my direct emailing list.

Members receive special offers and free bonus coloring sheets.

Now flip through this book and see what calls to you:
Which mandala will you color first?
Enjoy!

~ Marian

P.S. Don't forget to test first!
If you're using a wet medium like markers rather than a dry medium like colored pencils, remember to place a protective sheet between the page you're coloring and the next design, in case there's a bleed-through. You can use these squares for your test:

This side left intentionally blank.

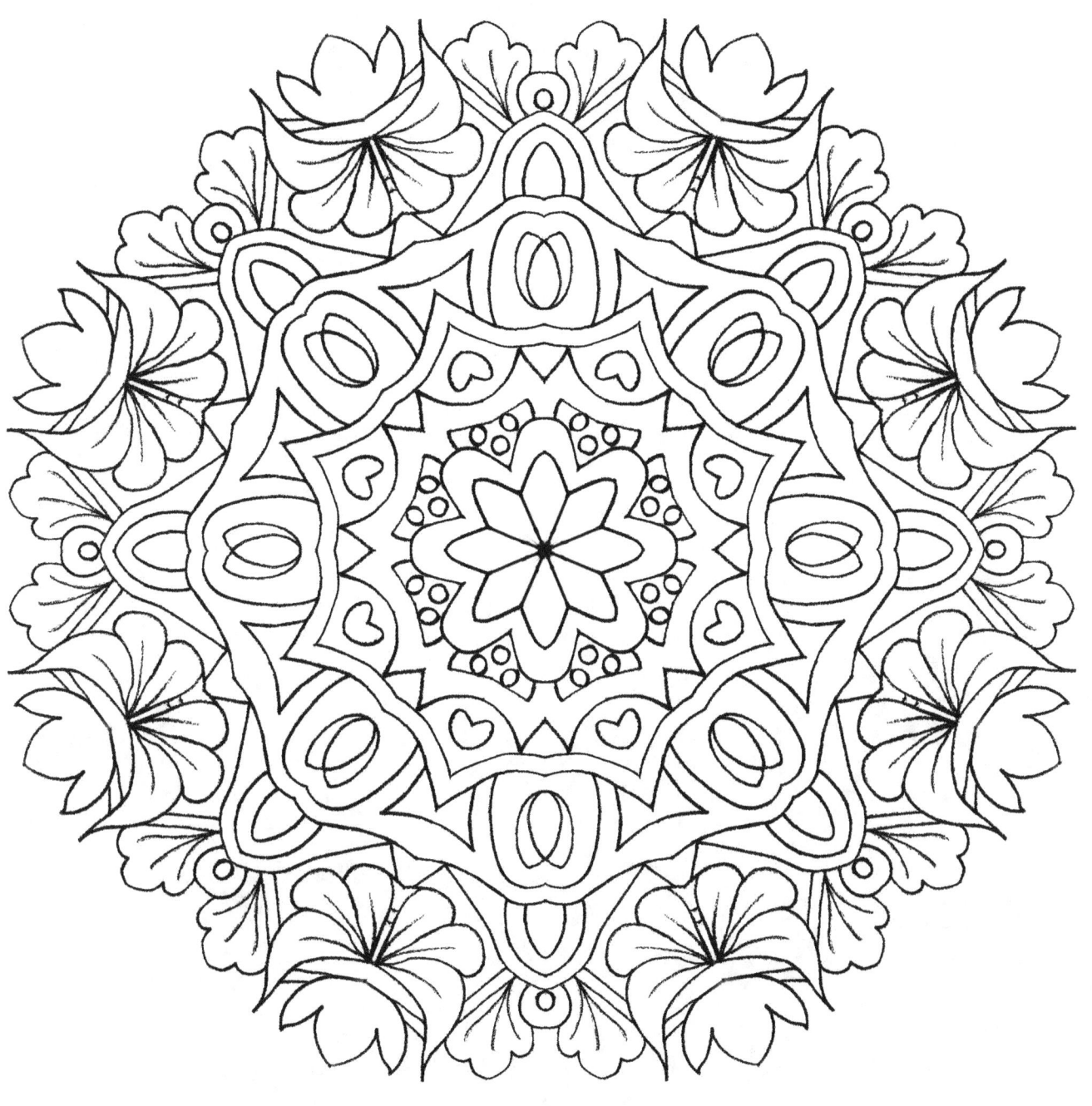

p.5   Colored by_____

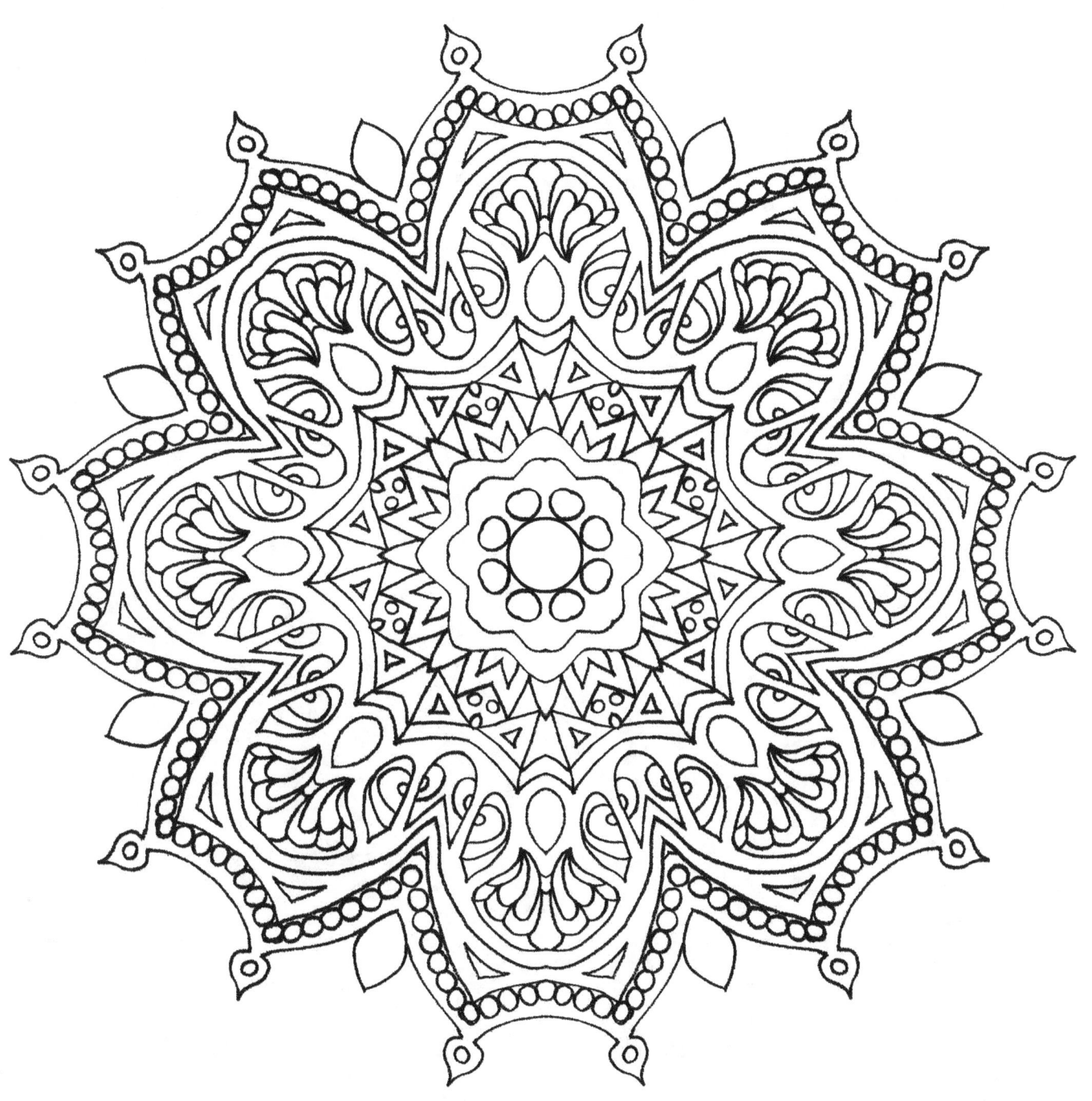

This side left intentionally blank.

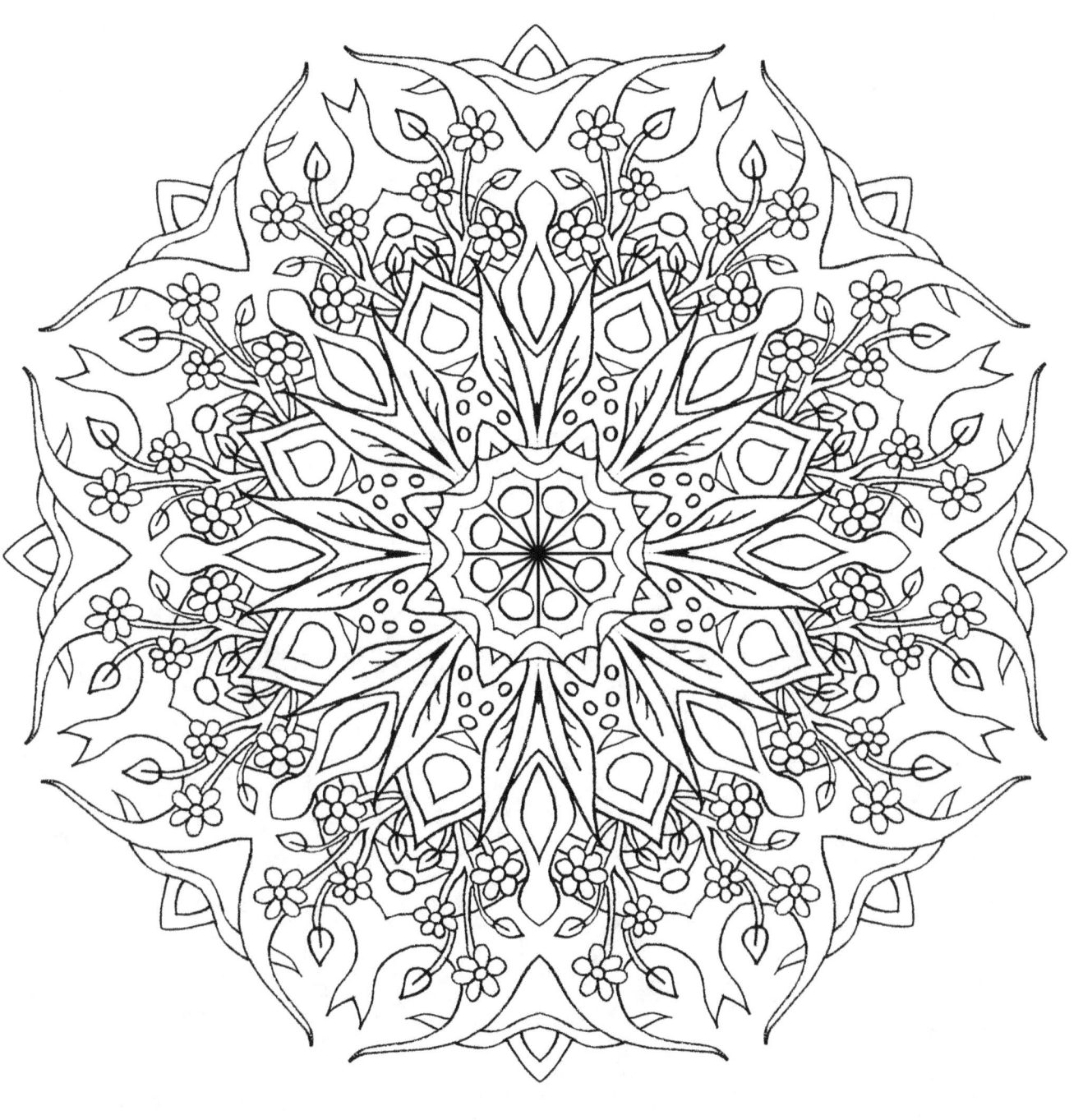

p.9   Colored by_____

This side left intentionally blank.

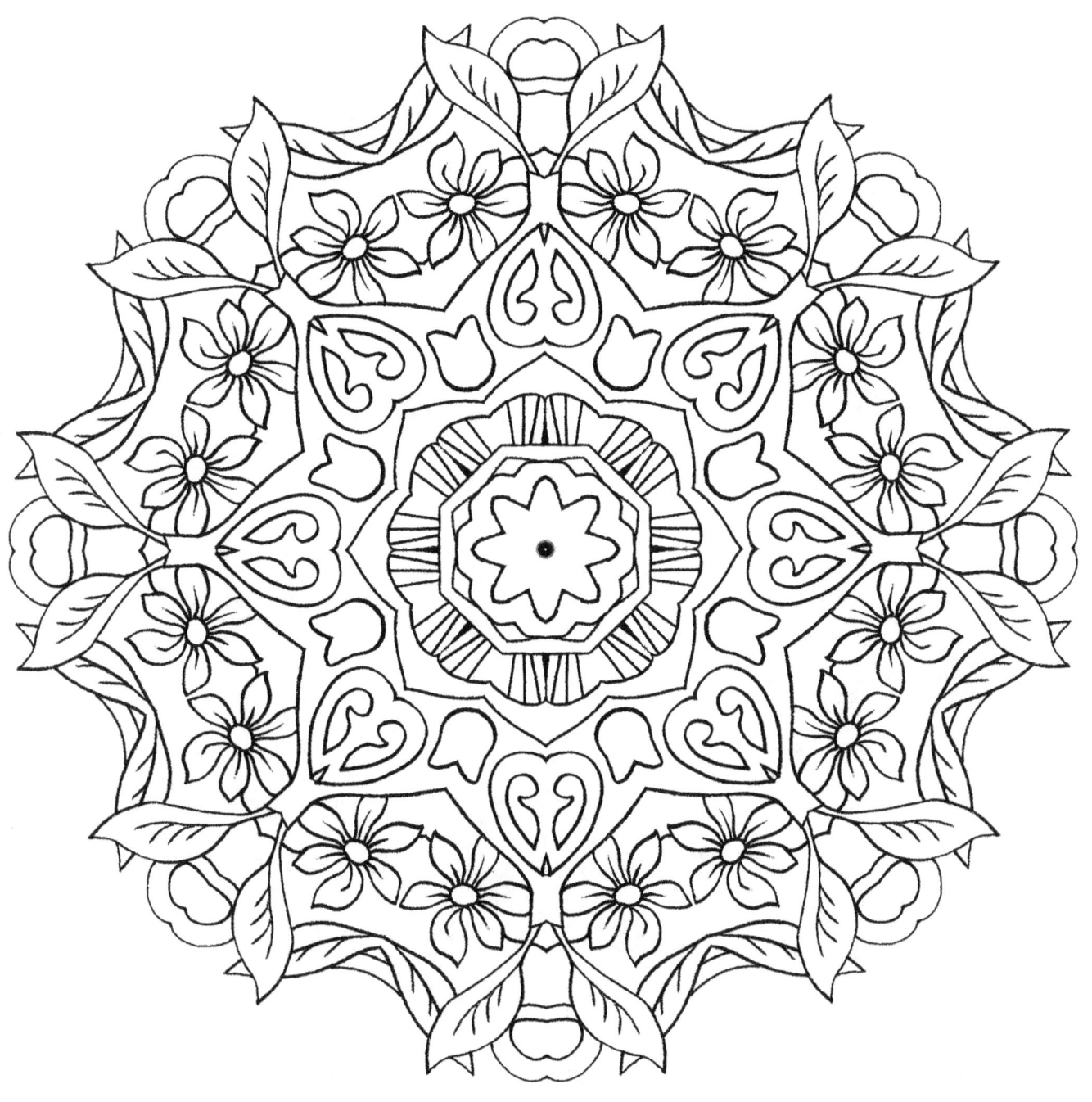

This side left intentionally blank.

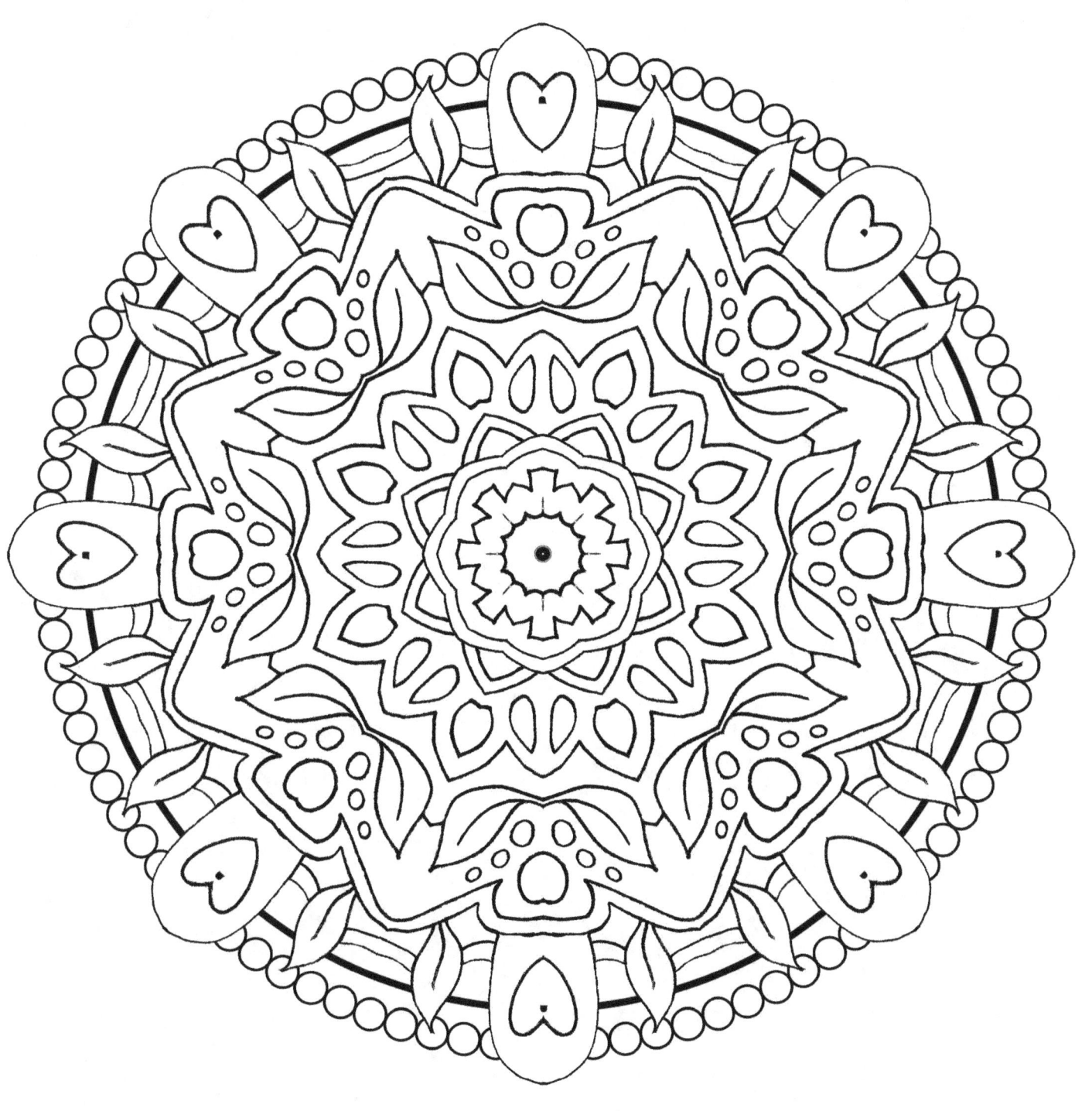

Design copyright © 2016 Marian Buchanan   p.13   Colored by_____

This side left intentionally blank.

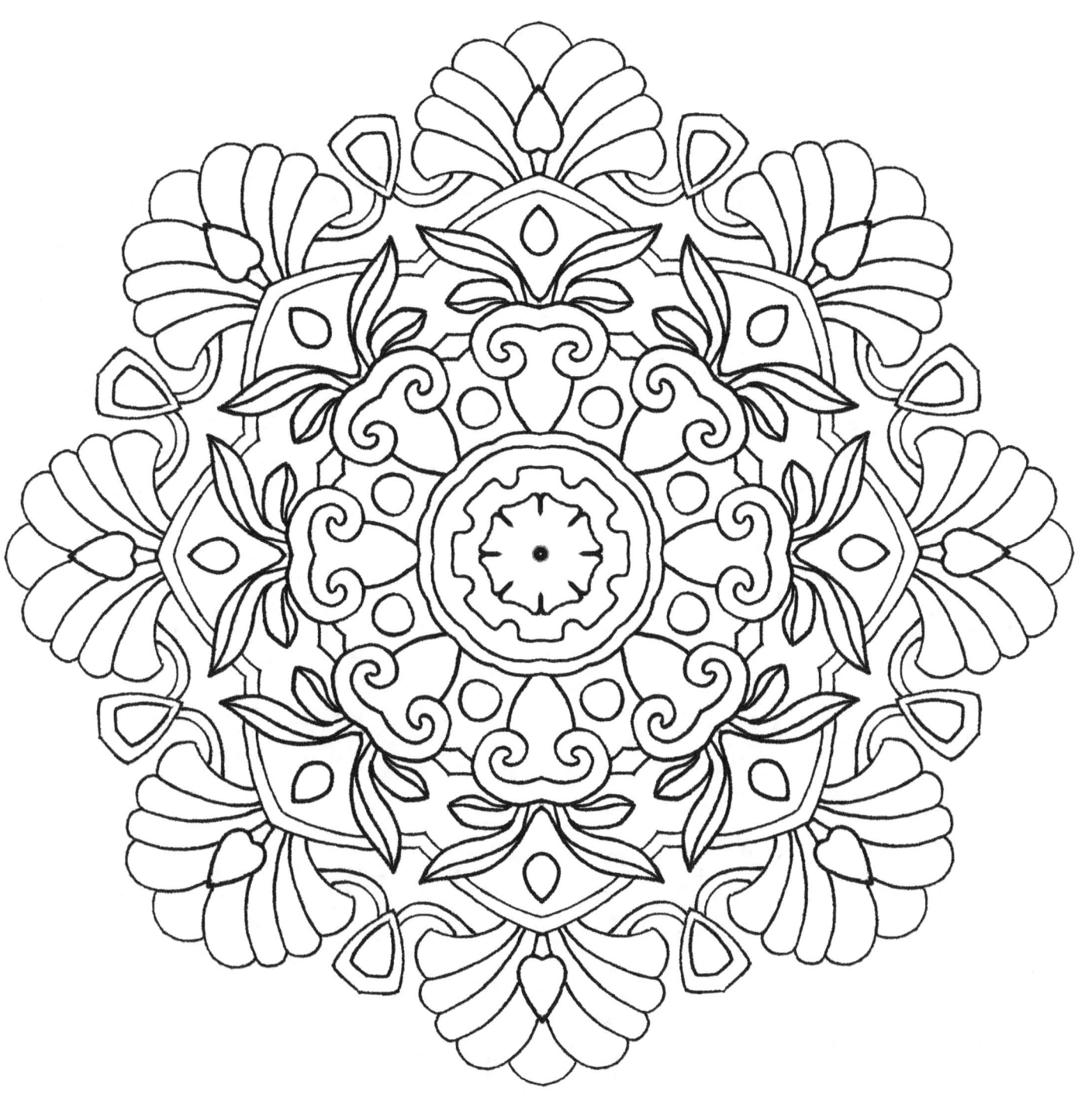

p.15   Colored by_____

This side left intentionally blank.

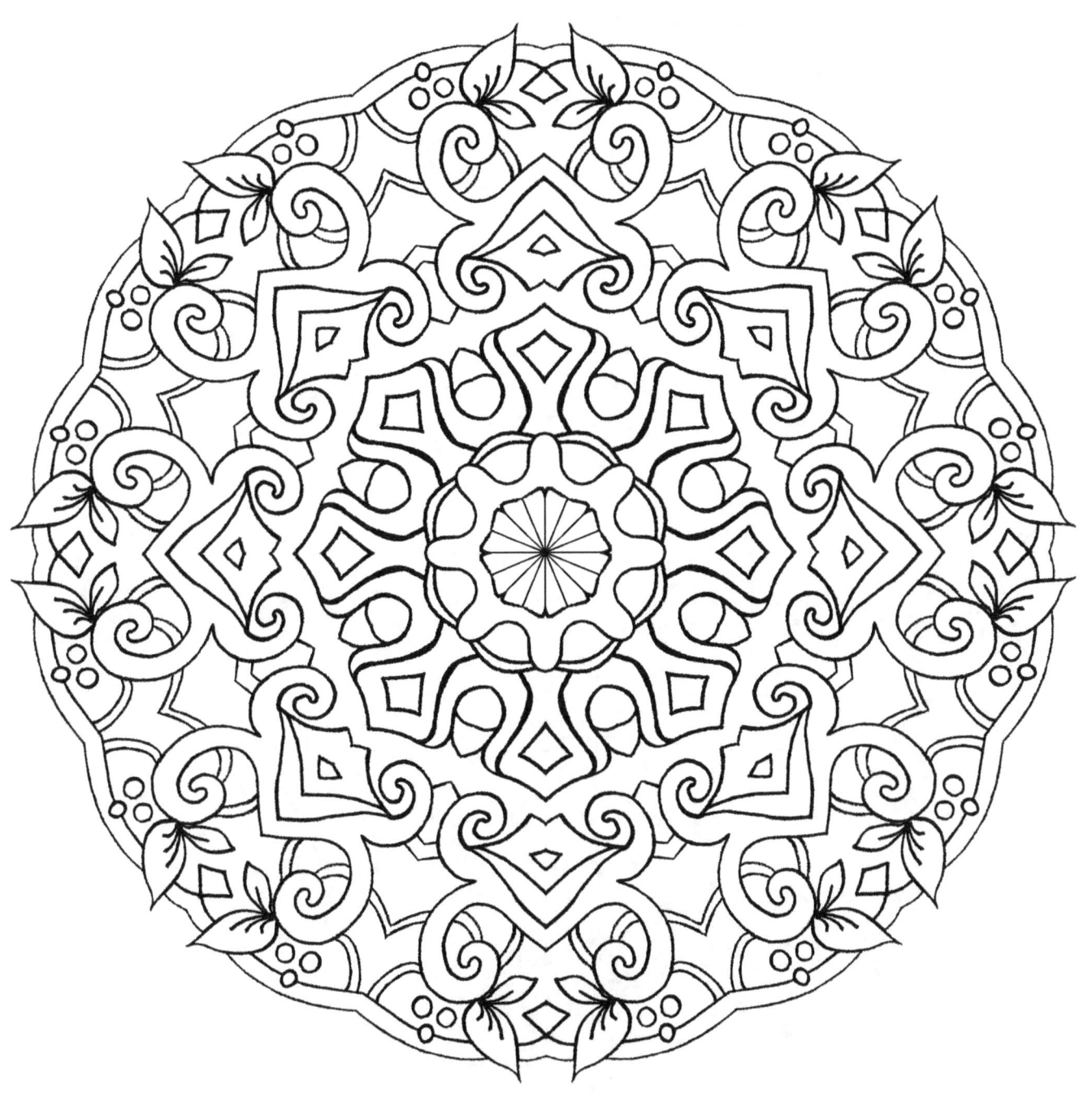

p.17   Colored by_____

This side left intentionally blank.

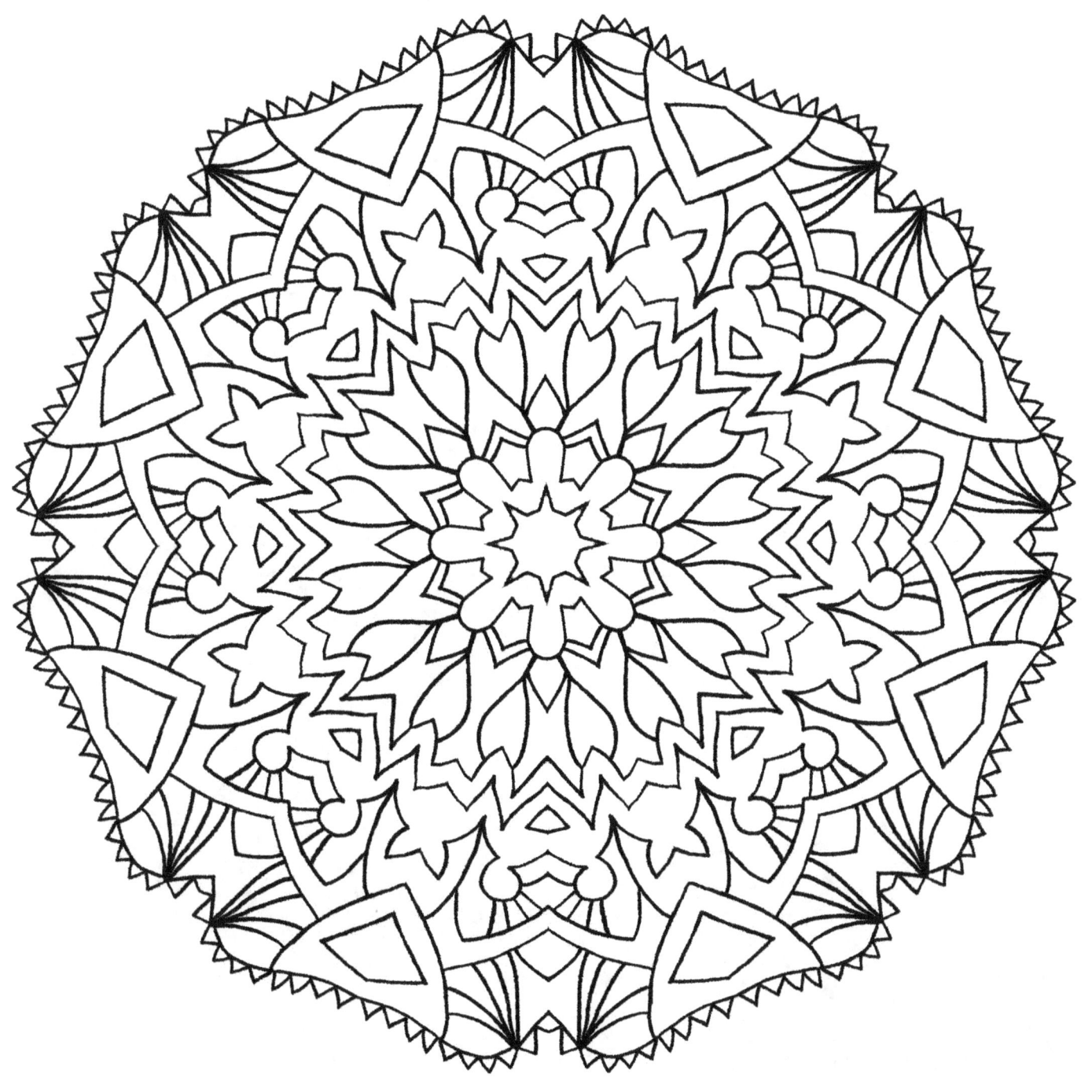

p.19   Colored by_____

This side left intentionally blank.

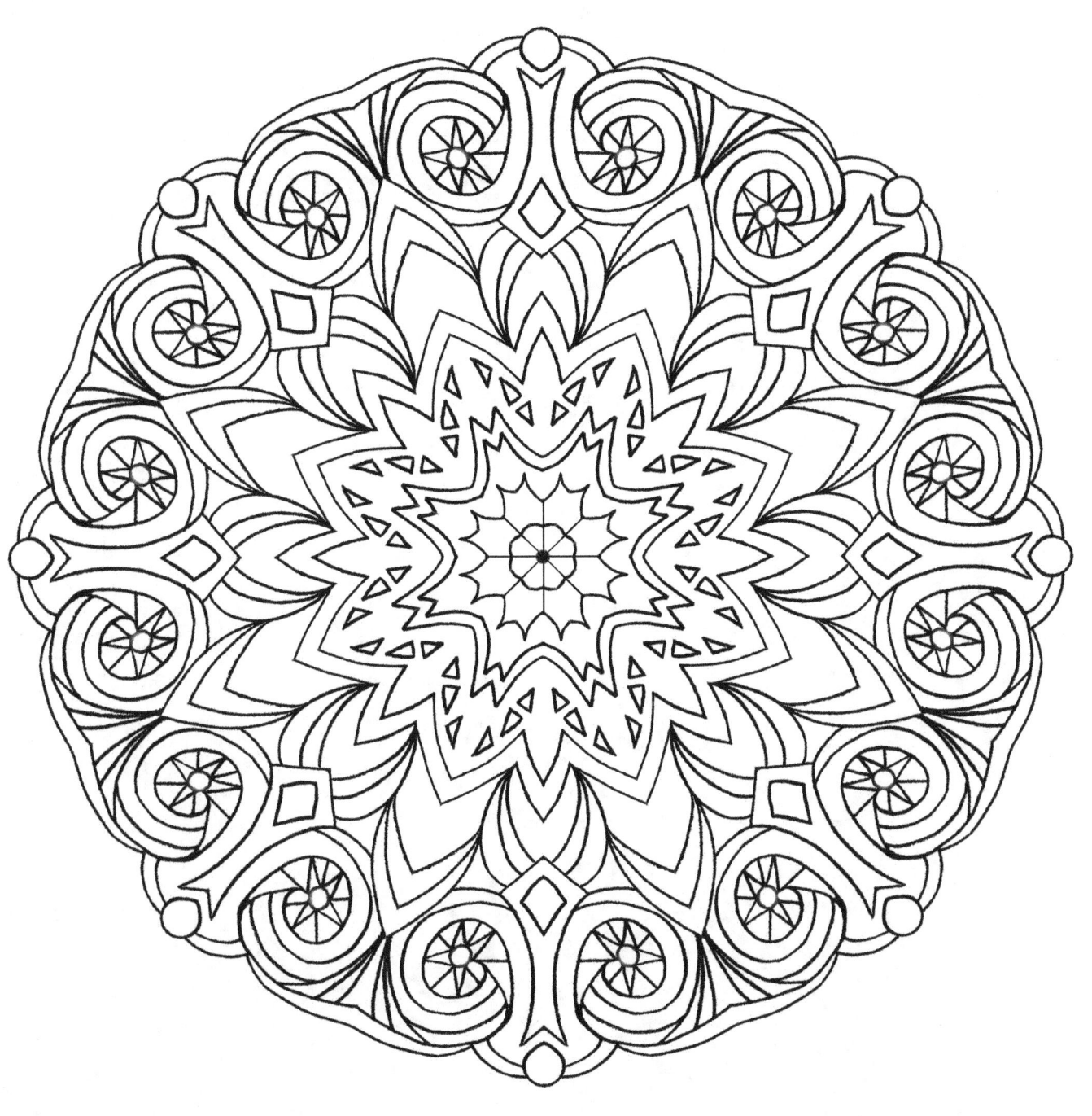

p.21   Colored by_____

This side left intentionally blank.

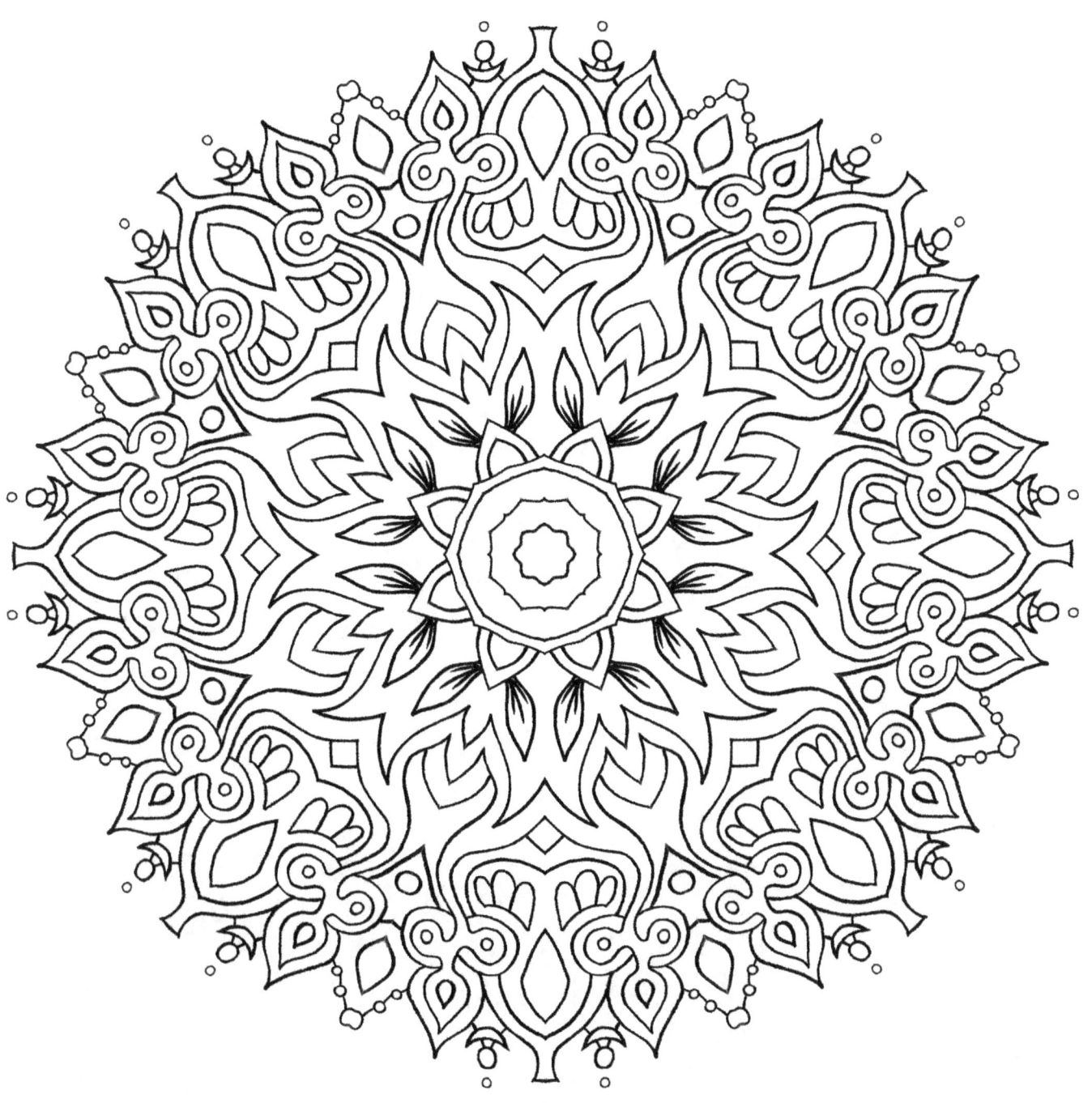

This side left intentionally blank.

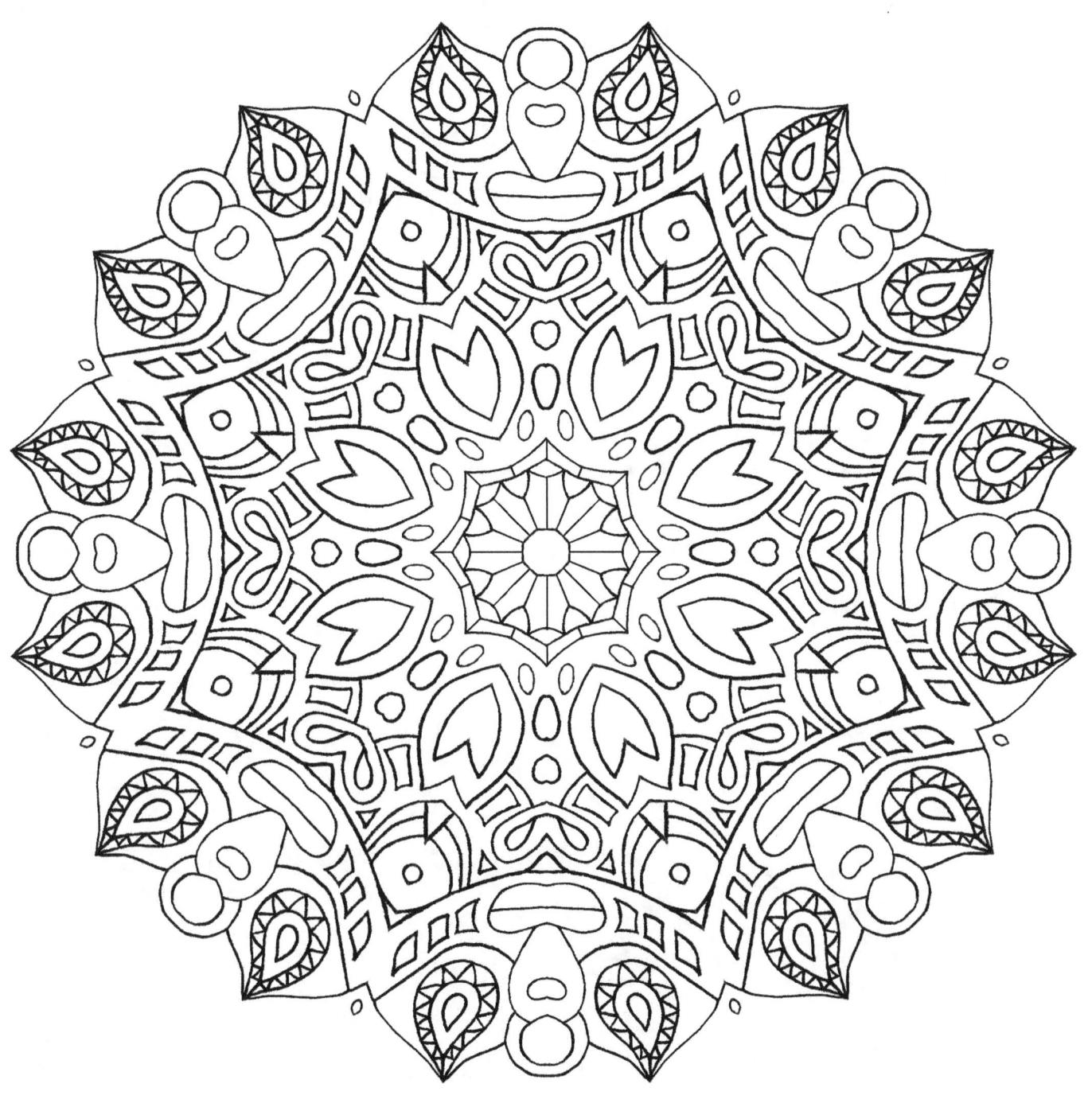

p.25   Colored by_____

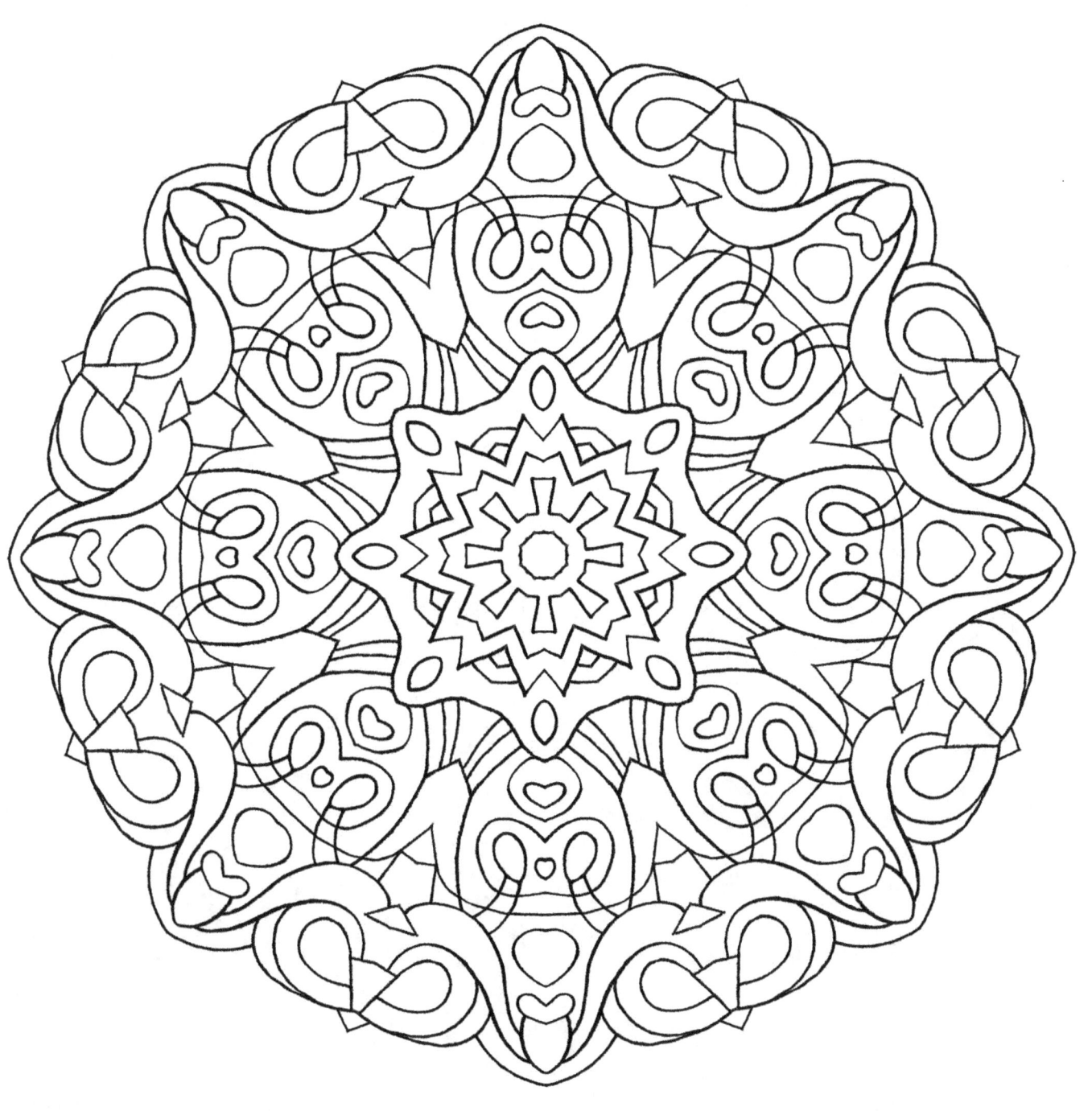

p.27 Colored by_____

This side left intentionally blank.

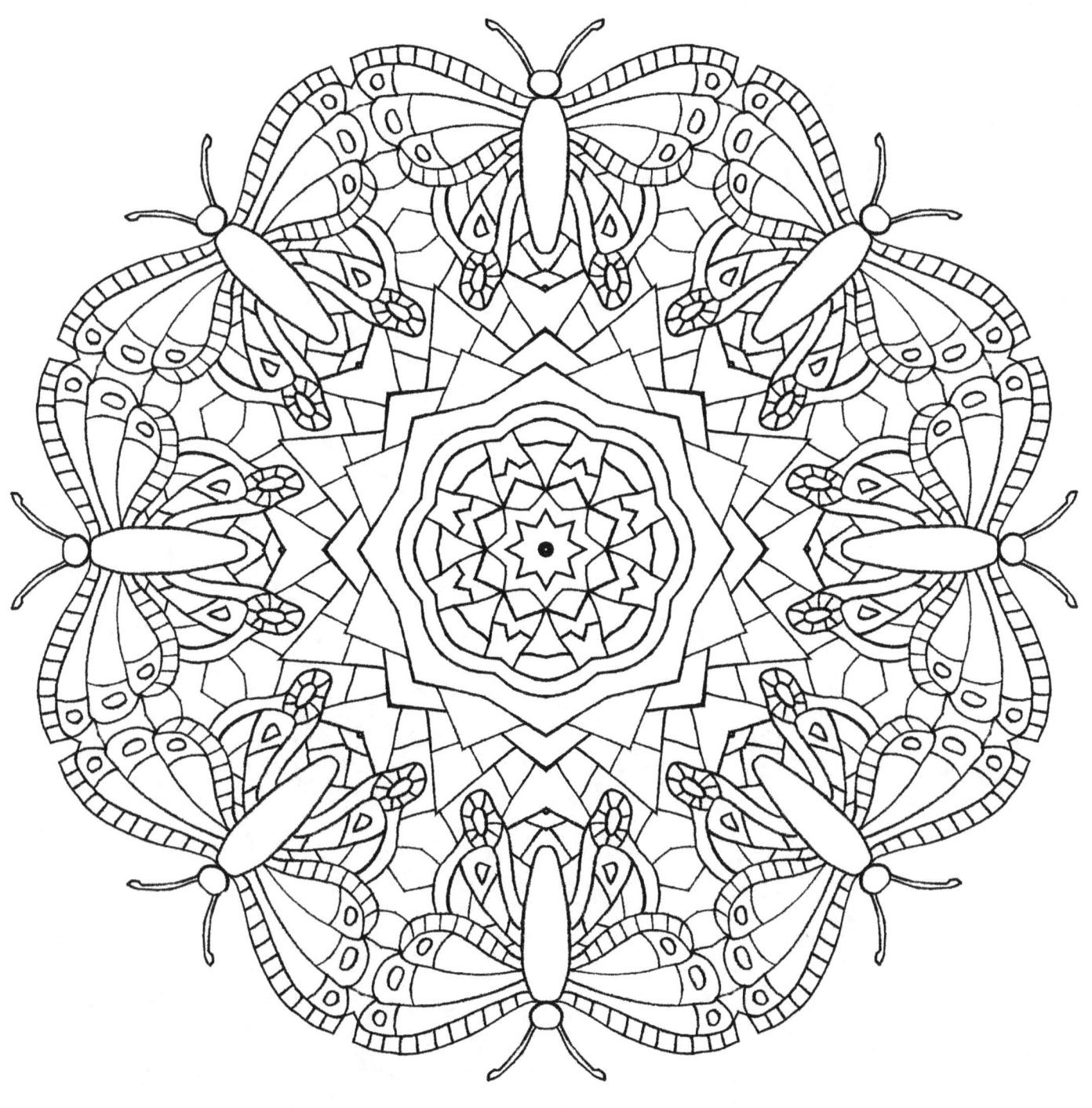

p.29   Colored by_____

This side left intentionally blank.

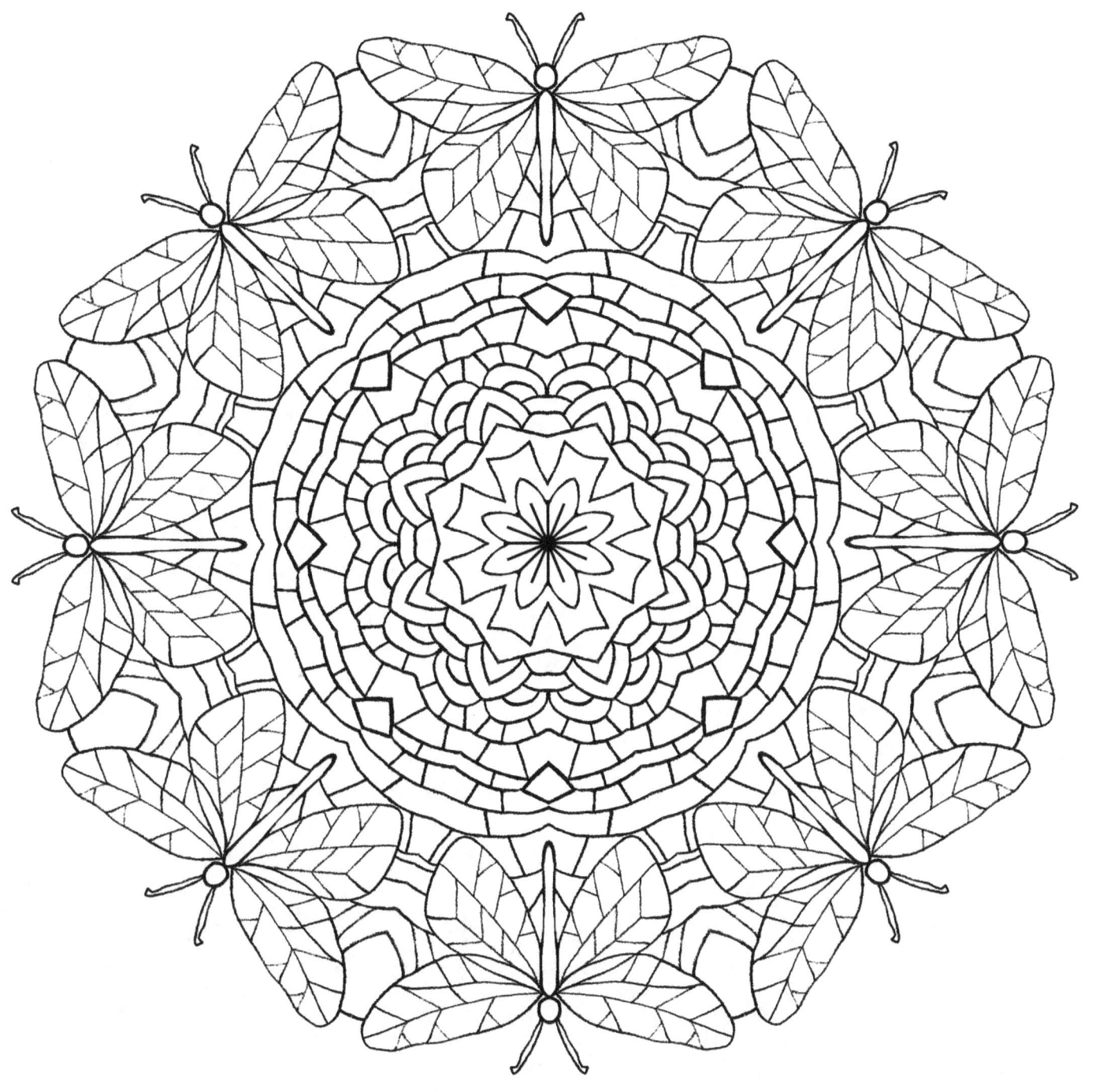

Design copyright © 2016 Marian Buchanan   p.31   Colored by_____

This side left intentionally blank.

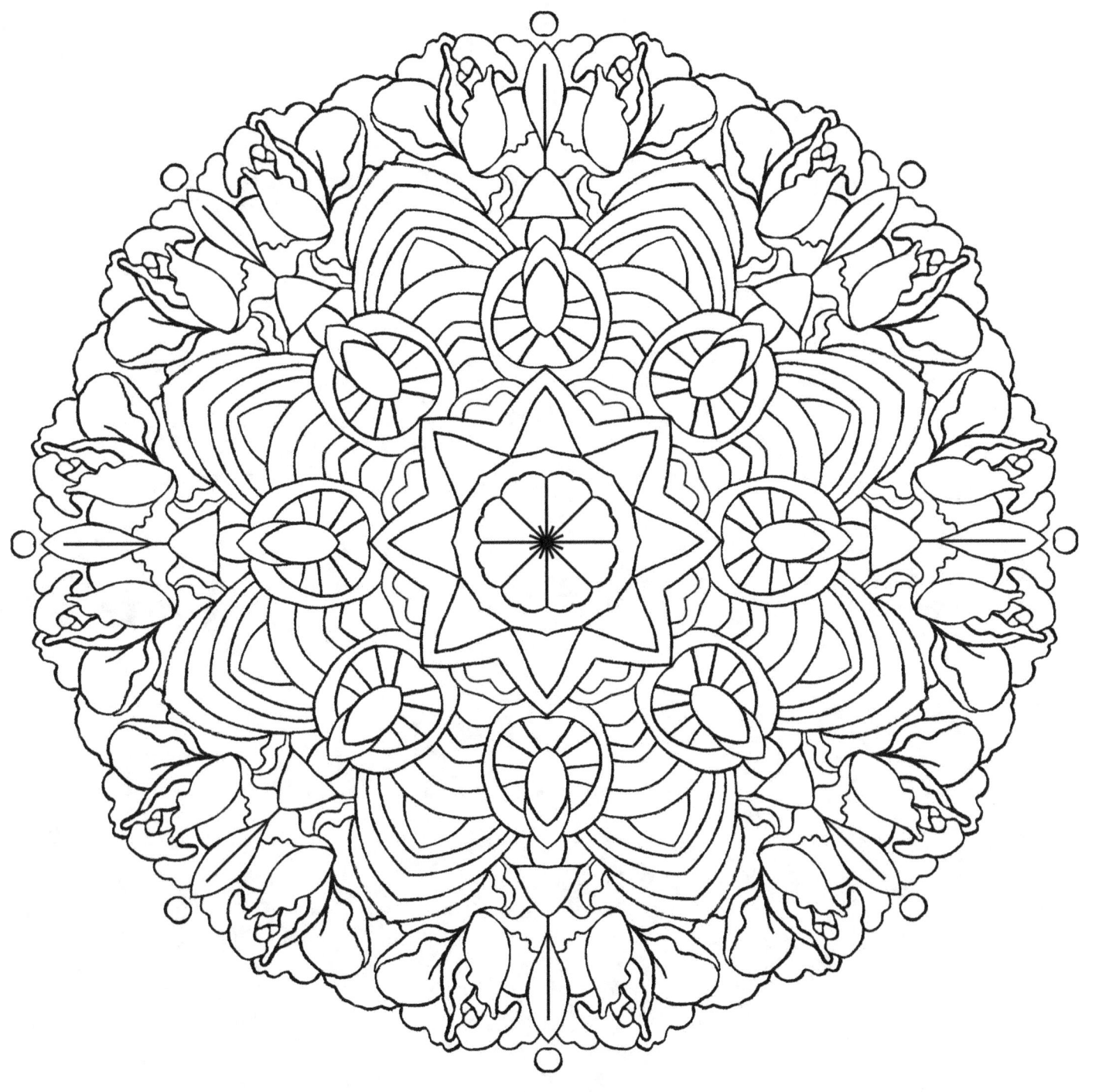

p.33   Colored by_____

This side left intentionally blank.

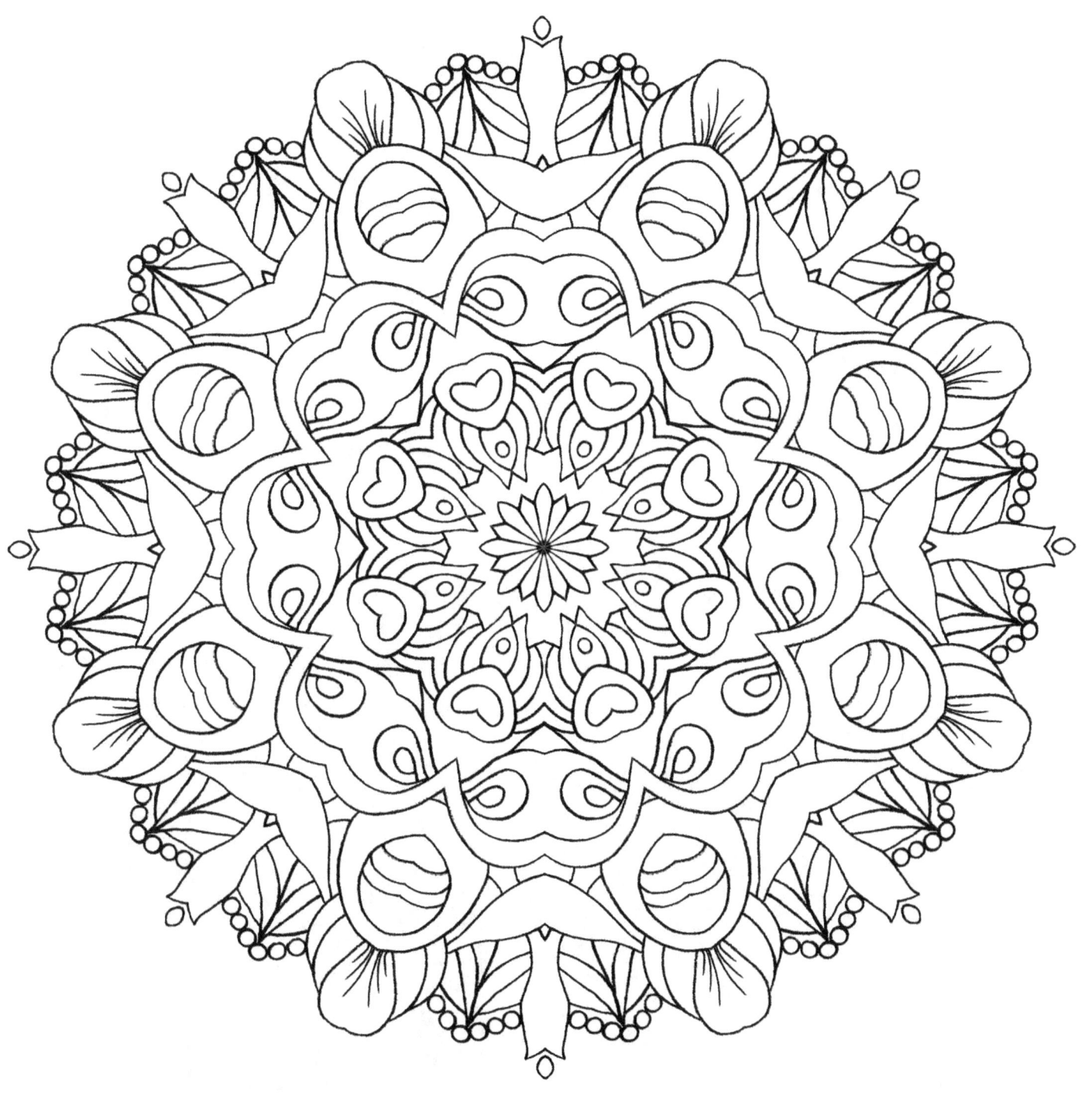

This side left intentionally blank.

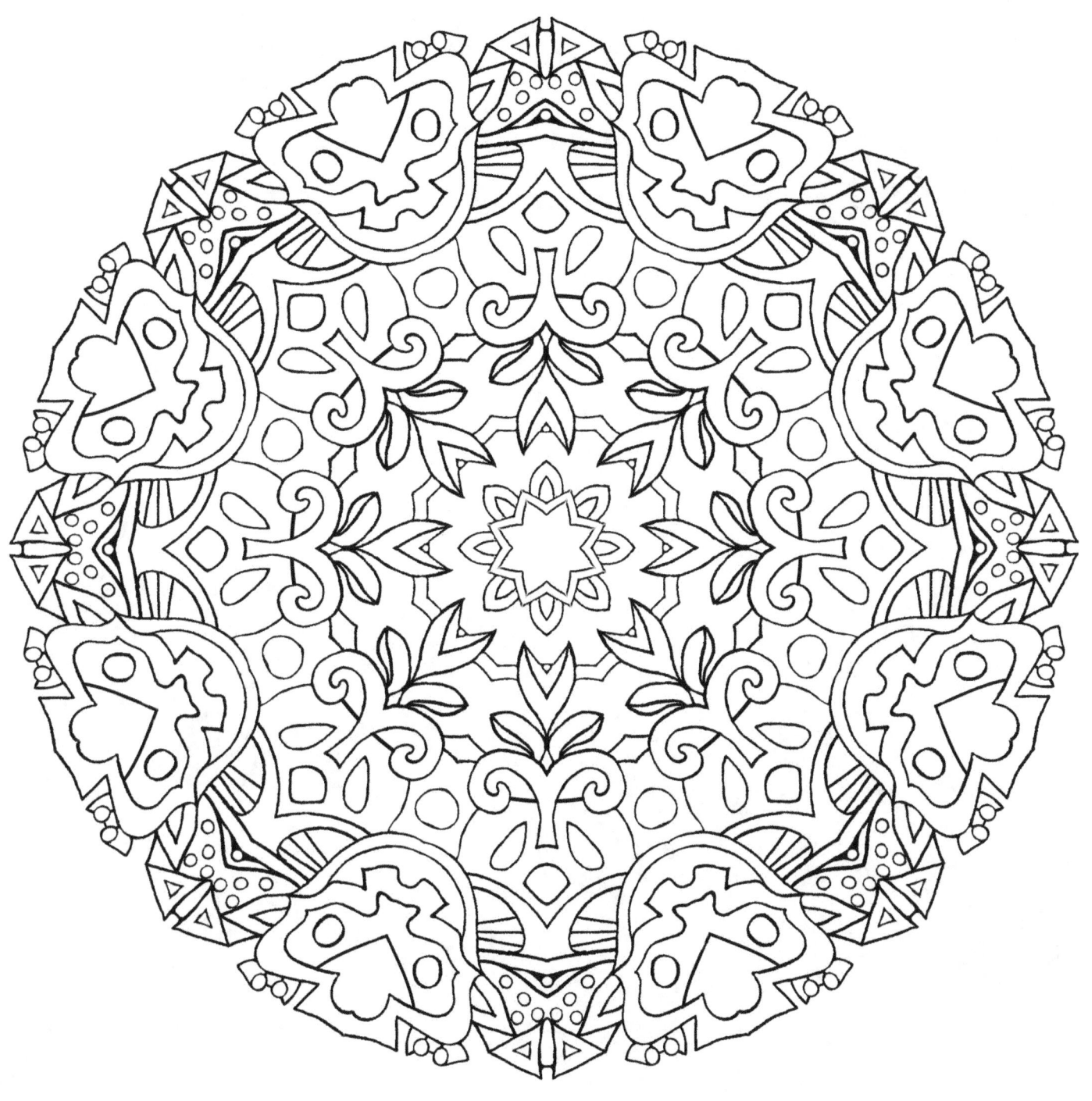

p.37   Colored by_____

This side left intentionally blank.

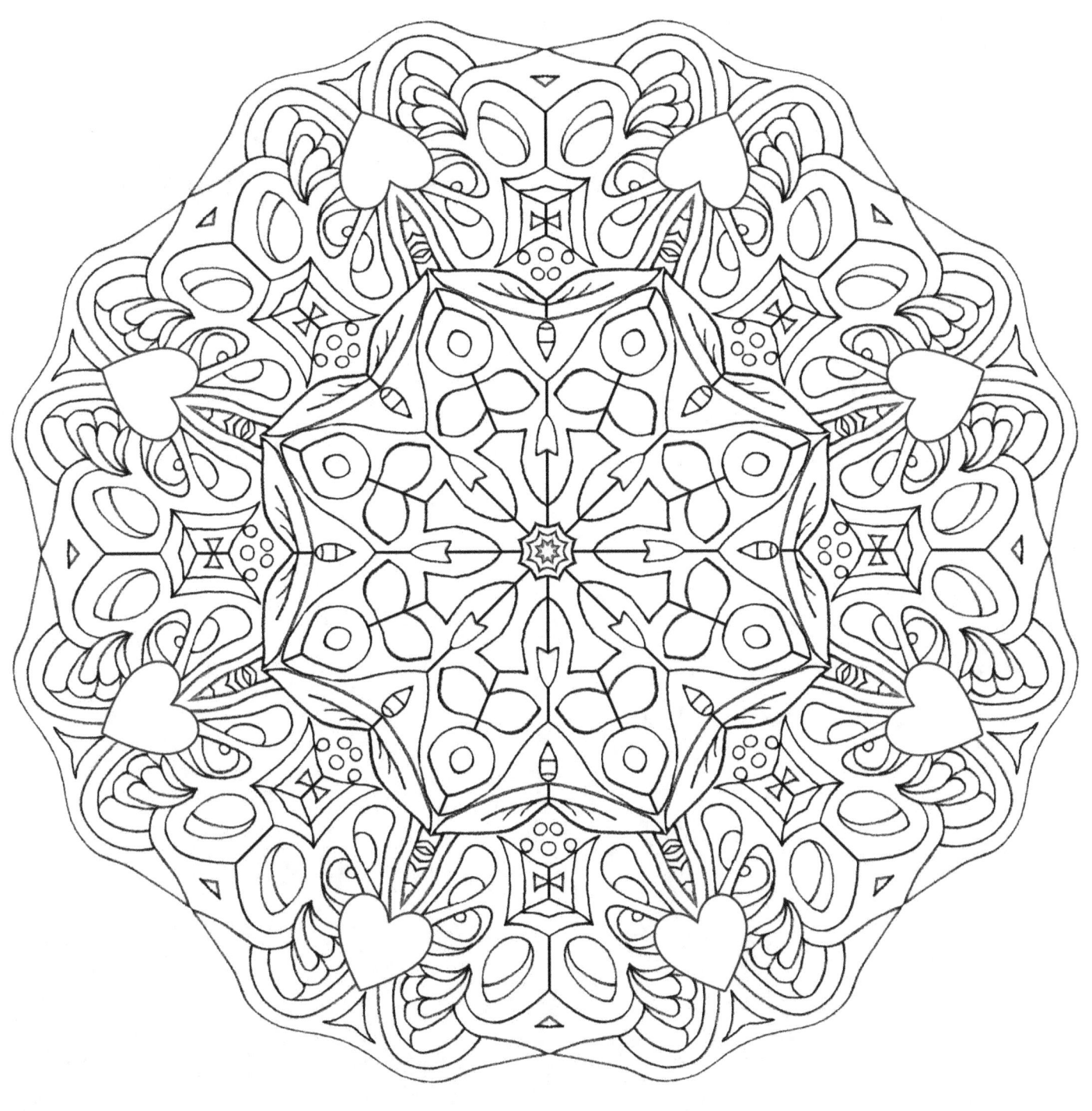

p.39   Colored by_____

This side left intentionally blank.

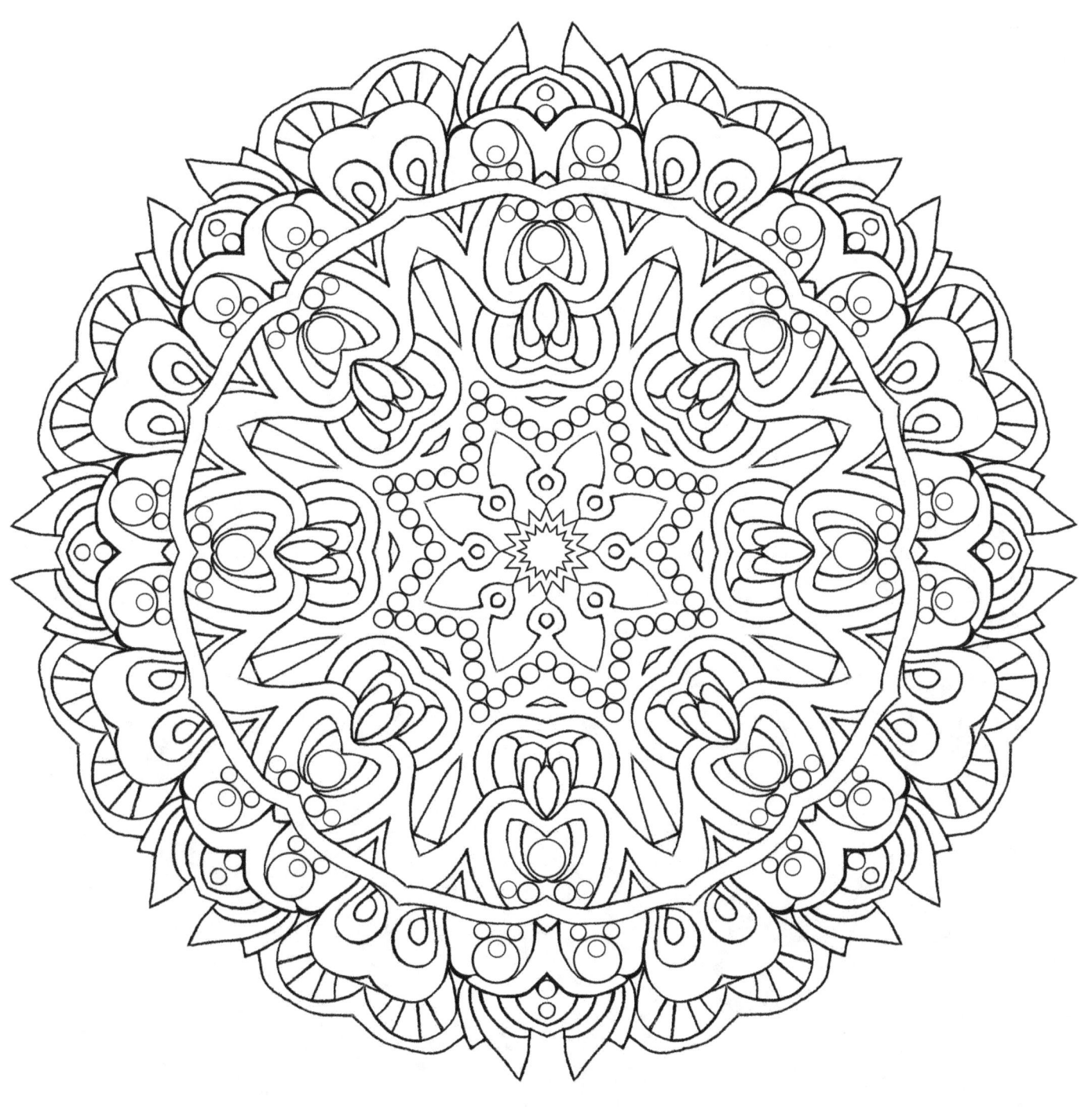

p.41   Colored by_____

This side left intentionally blank.

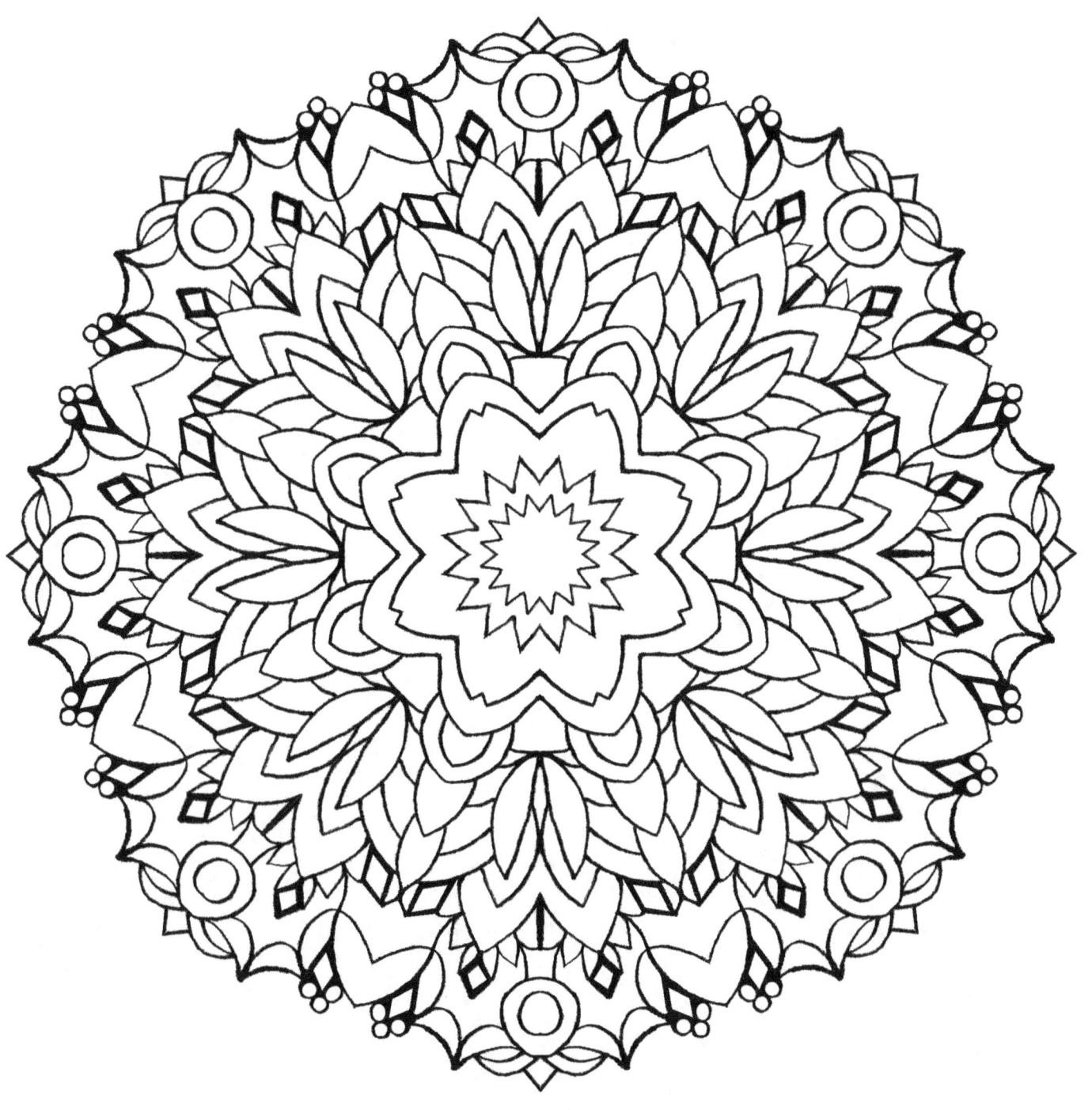

p.43 Colored by_____

This side left intentionally blank.

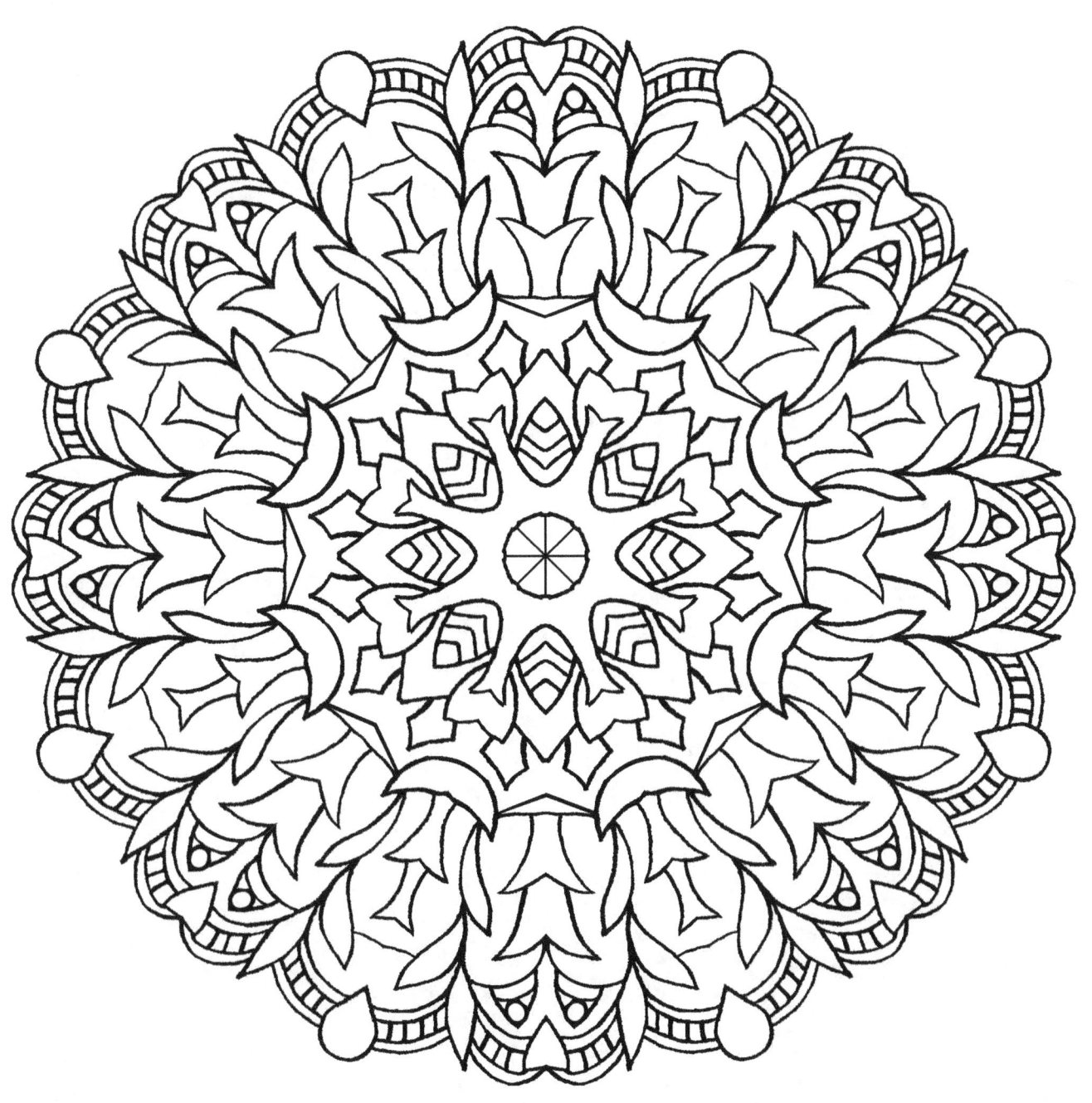

p.45 Colored by_____

This side left intentionally blank.

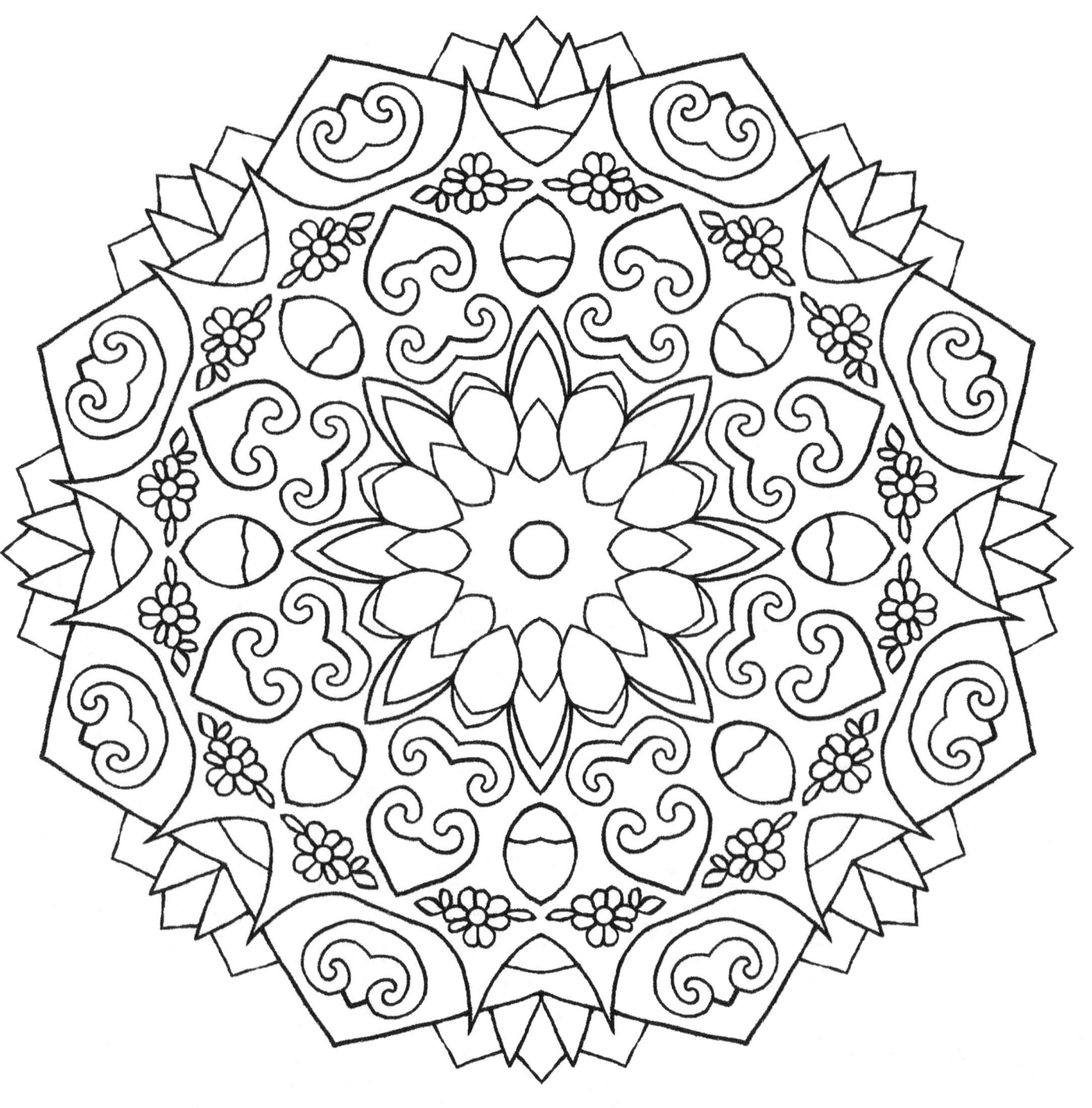

This side left intentionally blank.

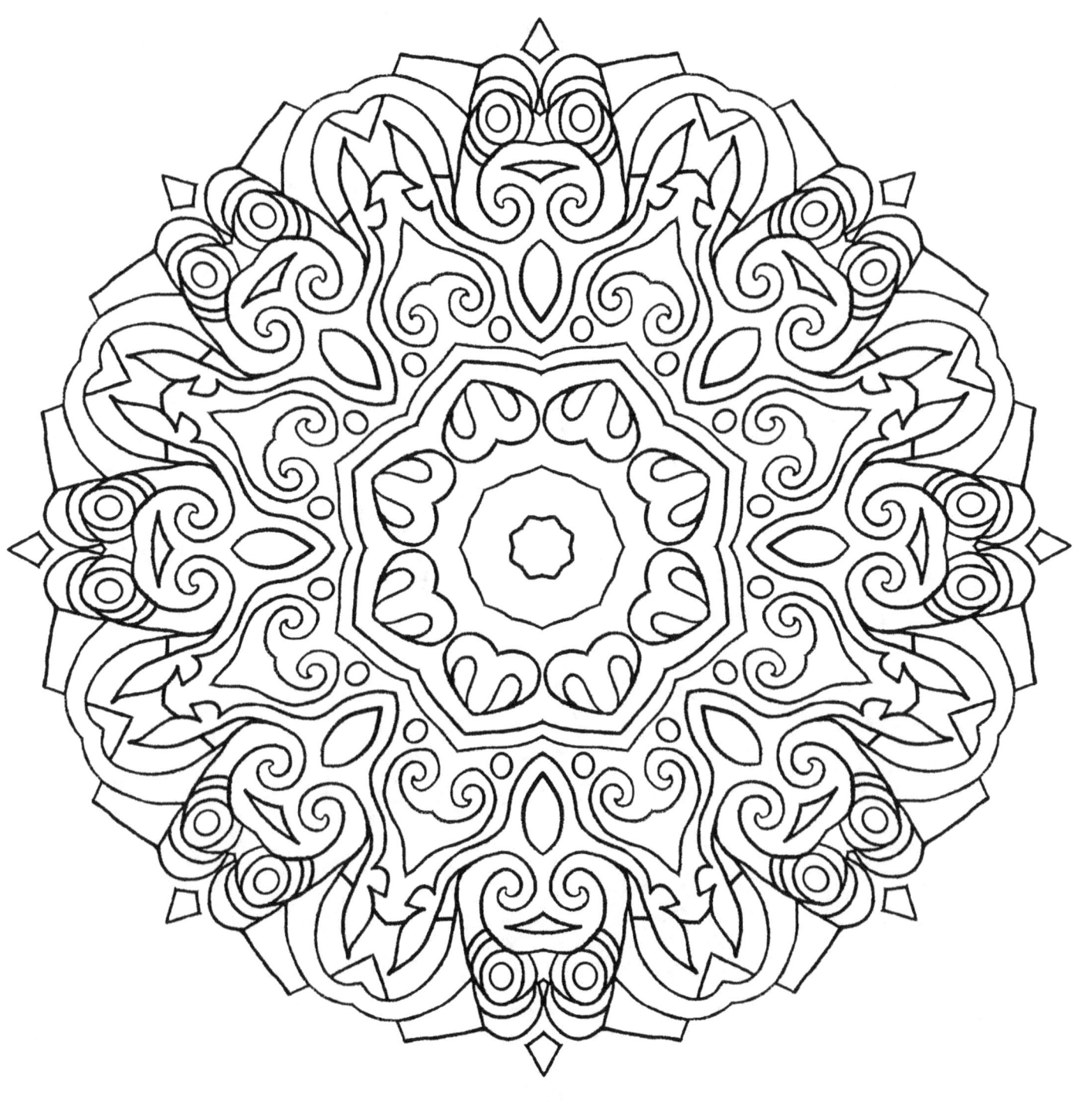

Design copyright © 2016 Marian Buchanan   p.49   Colored by_____

This side left intentionally blank.

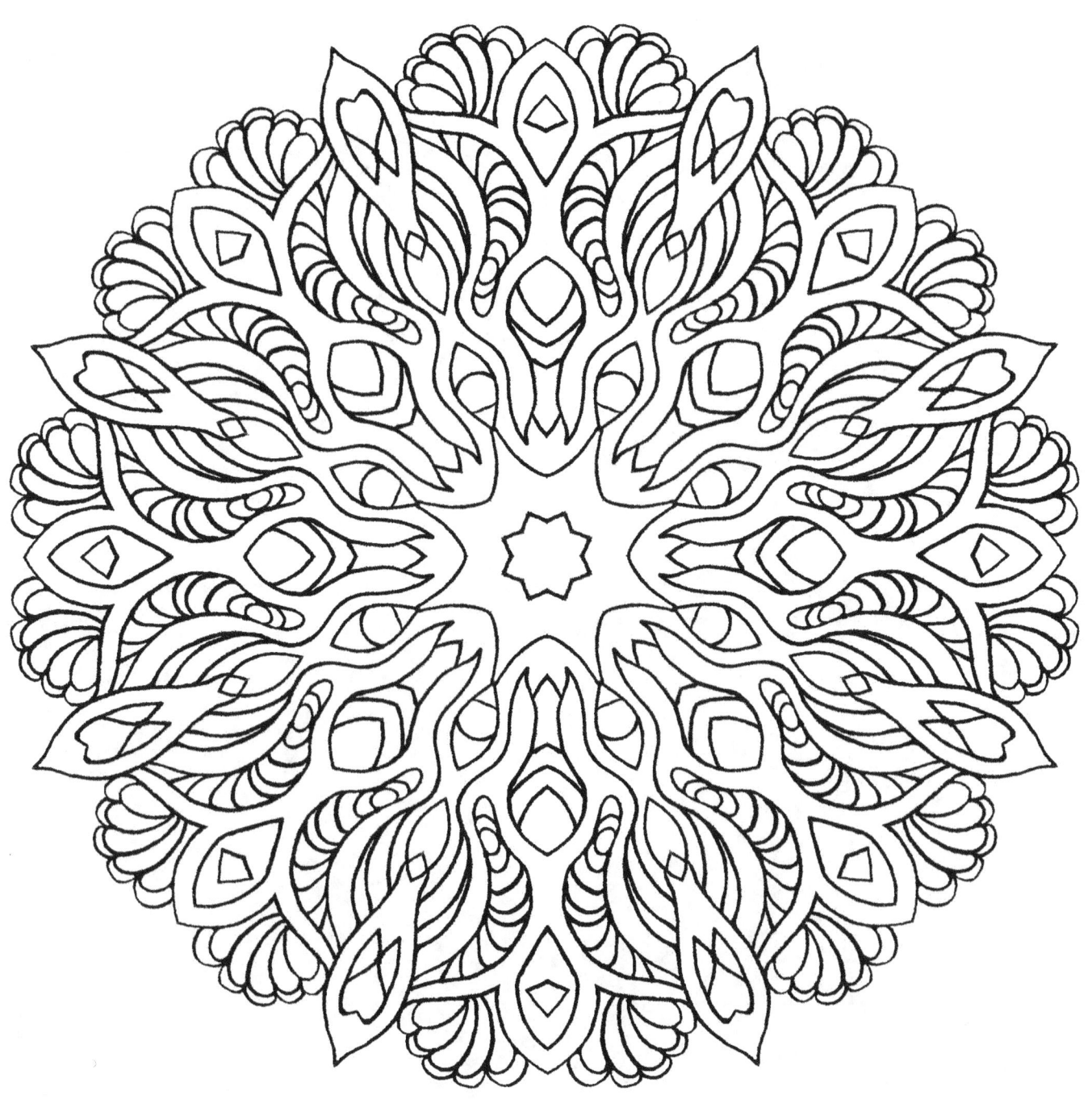

Design copyright © 2016 Marian Buchanan   p.51   Colored by_____

This side left intentionally blank.

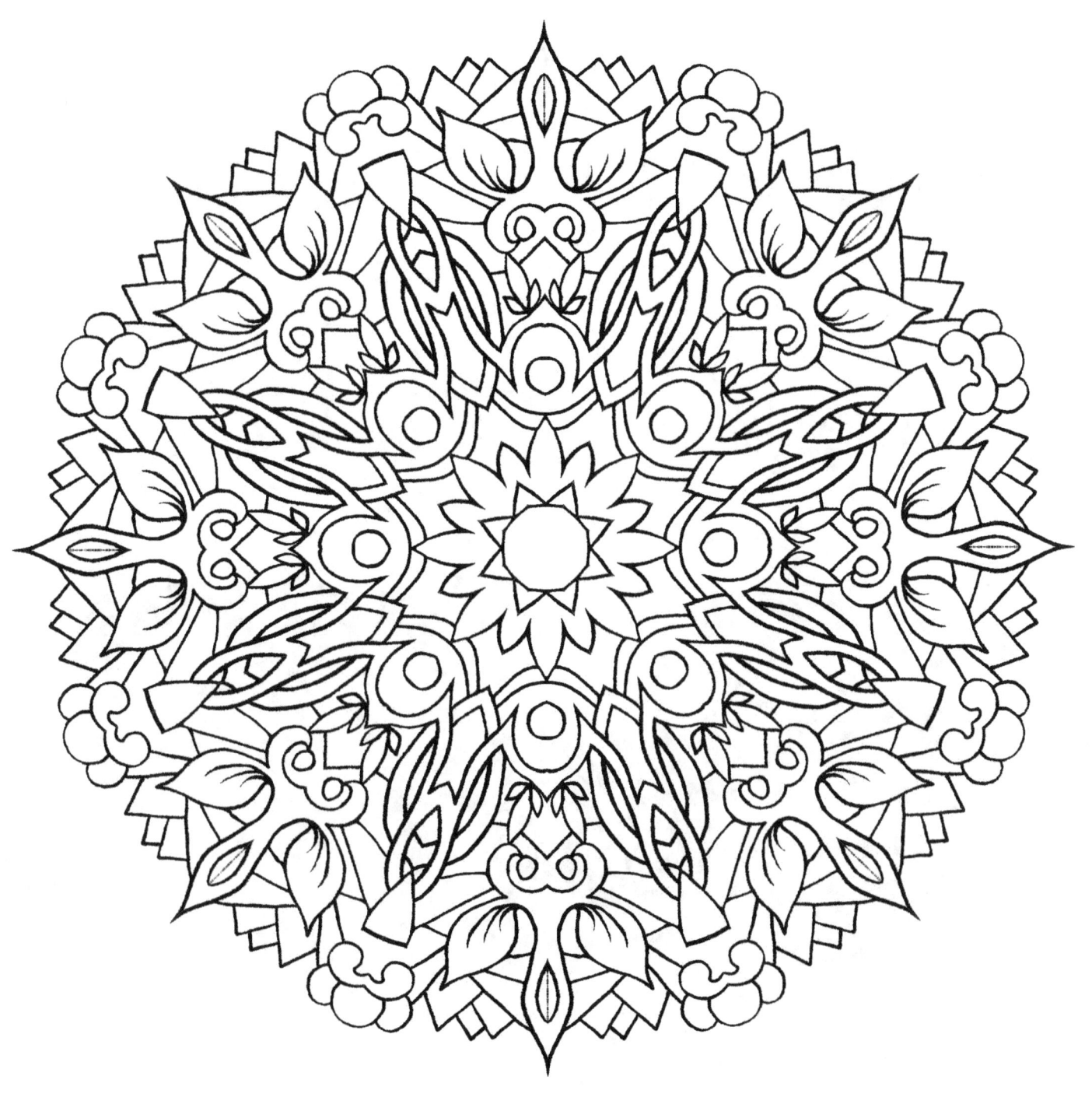

p.53   Colored by_____

This side left intentionally blank.

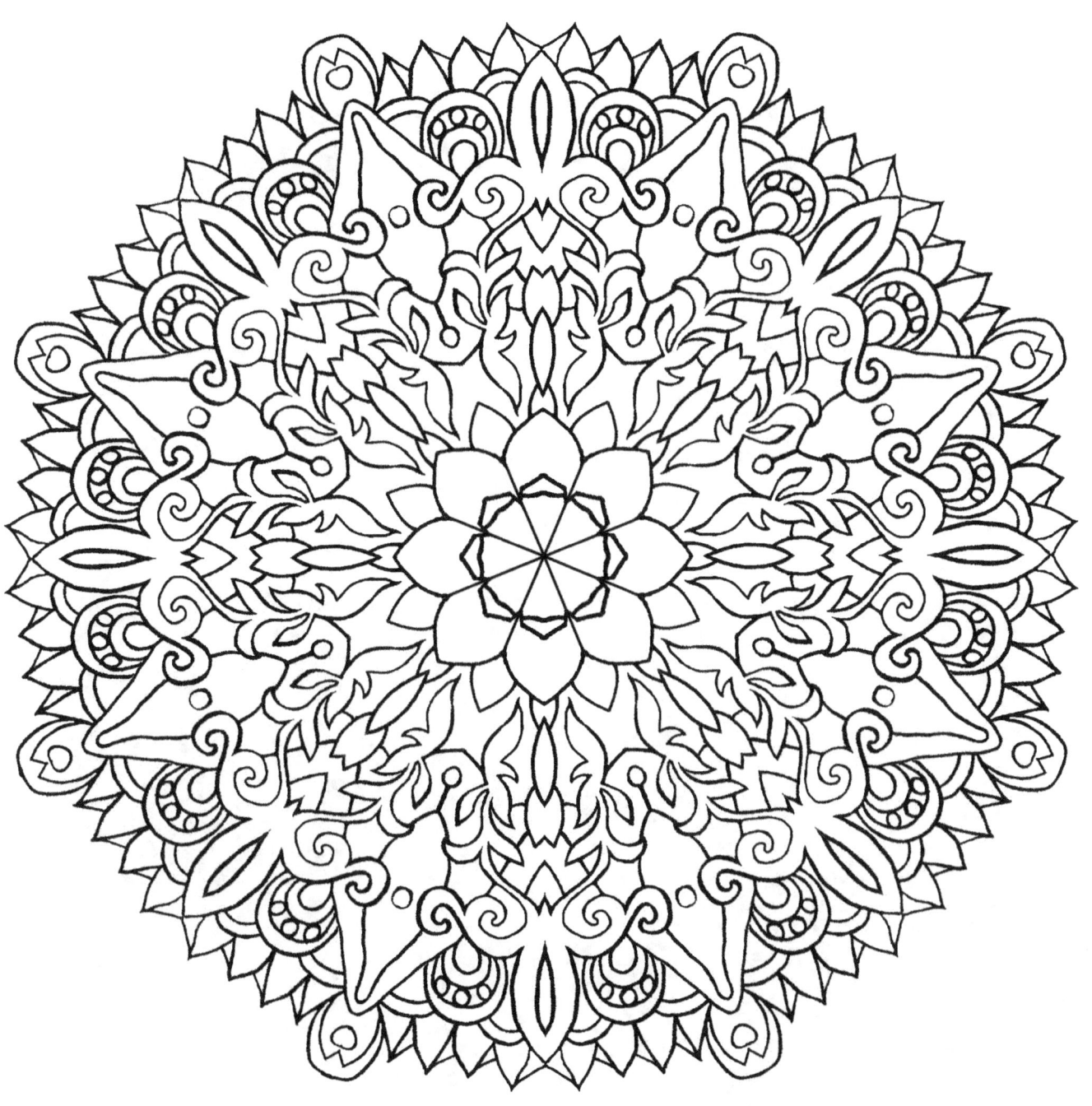

p.55   Colored by_____

This side left intentionally blank.

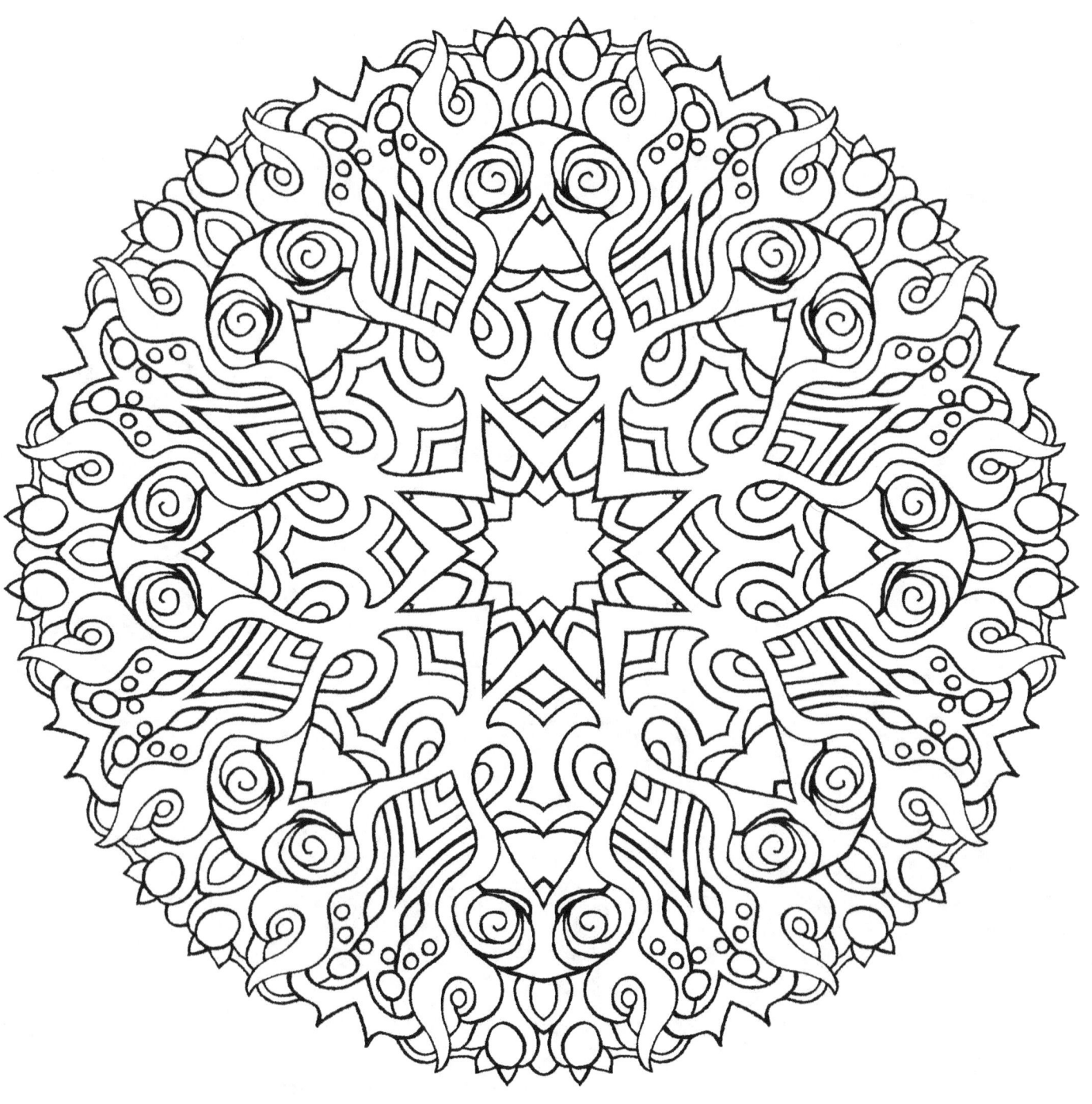

p.57   Colored by_____

This side left intentionally blank.

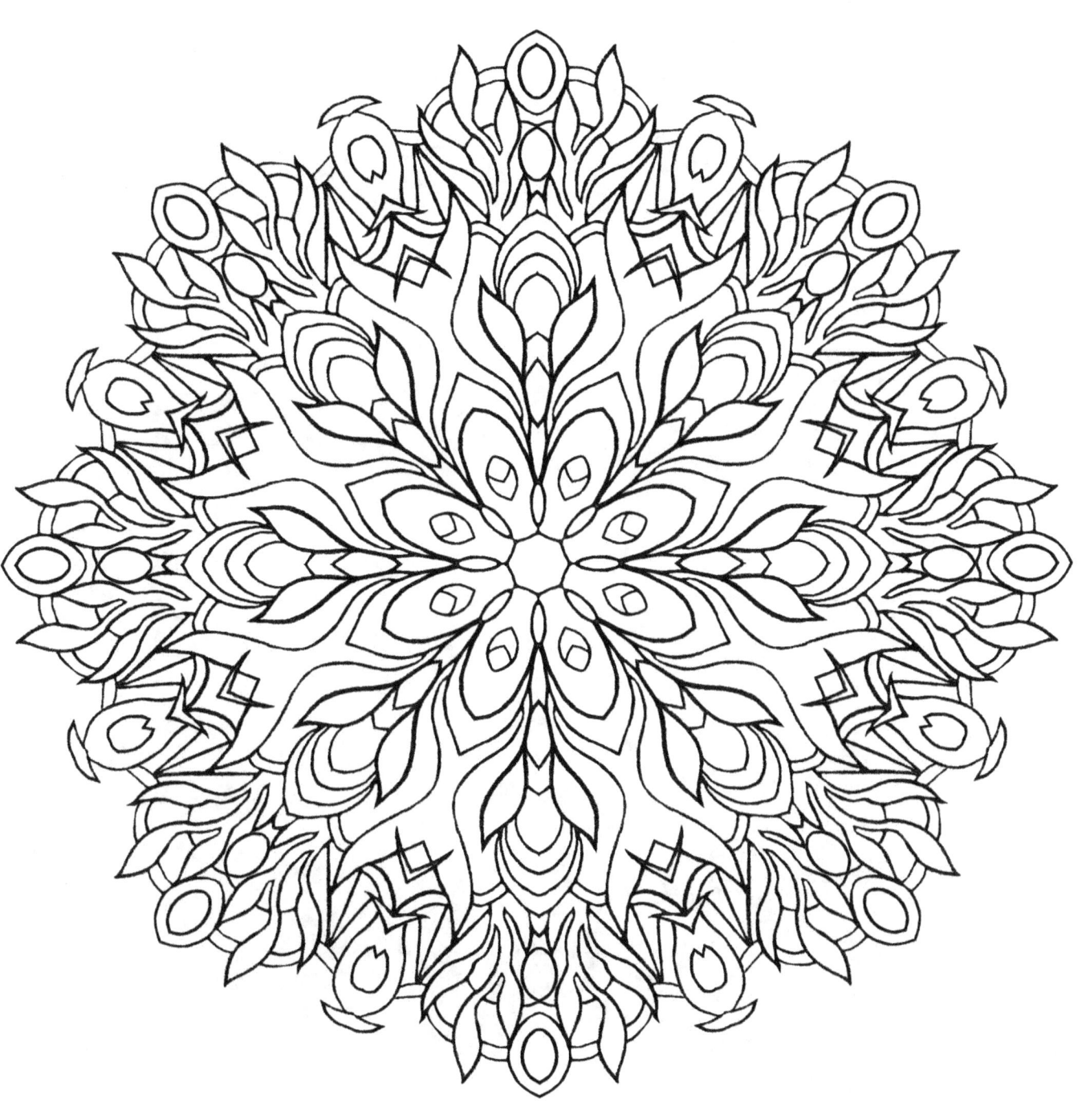

p.59   Colored by_____

This side left intentionally blank.

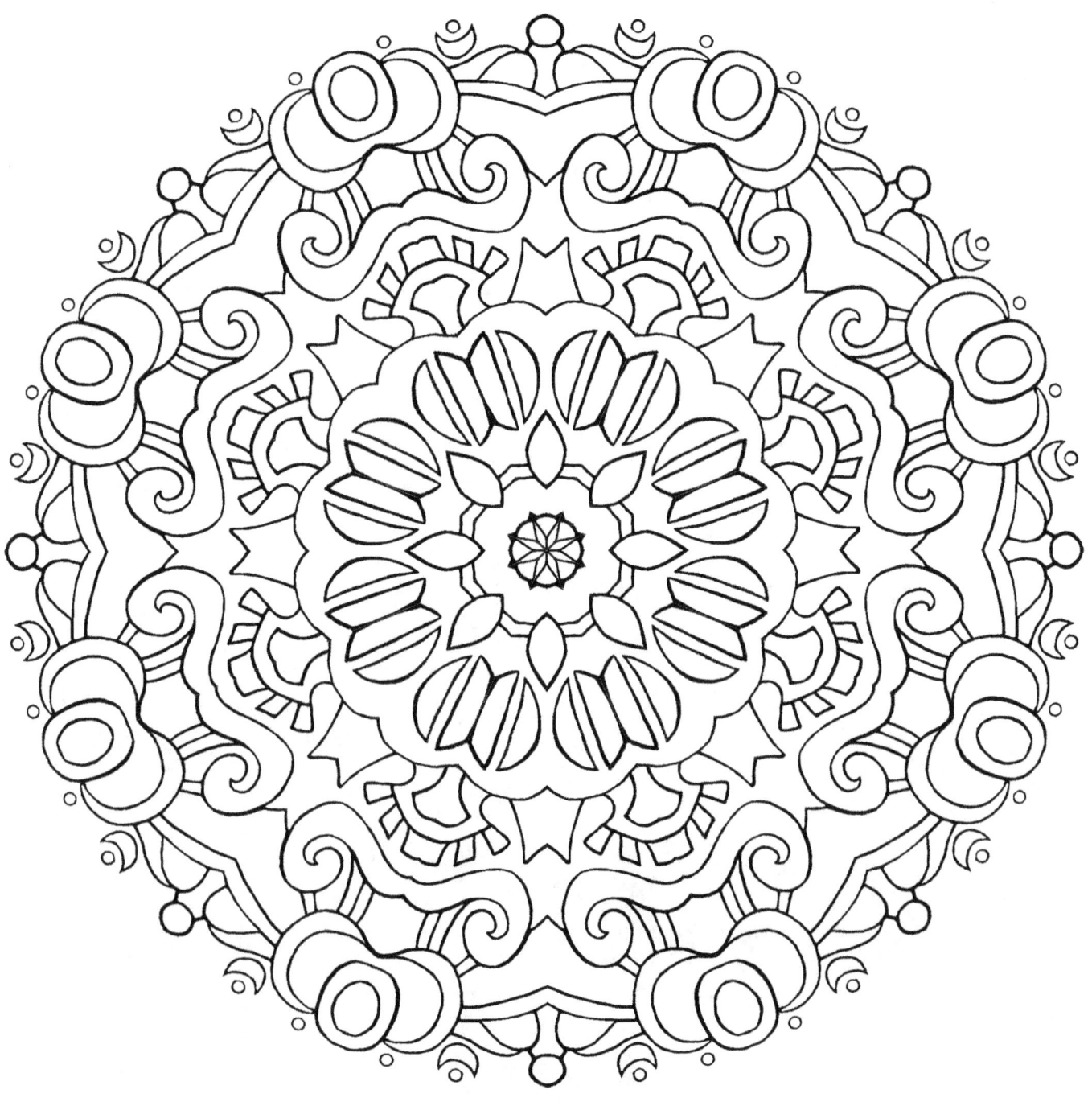

         Colored by_____

This side left intentionally blank.

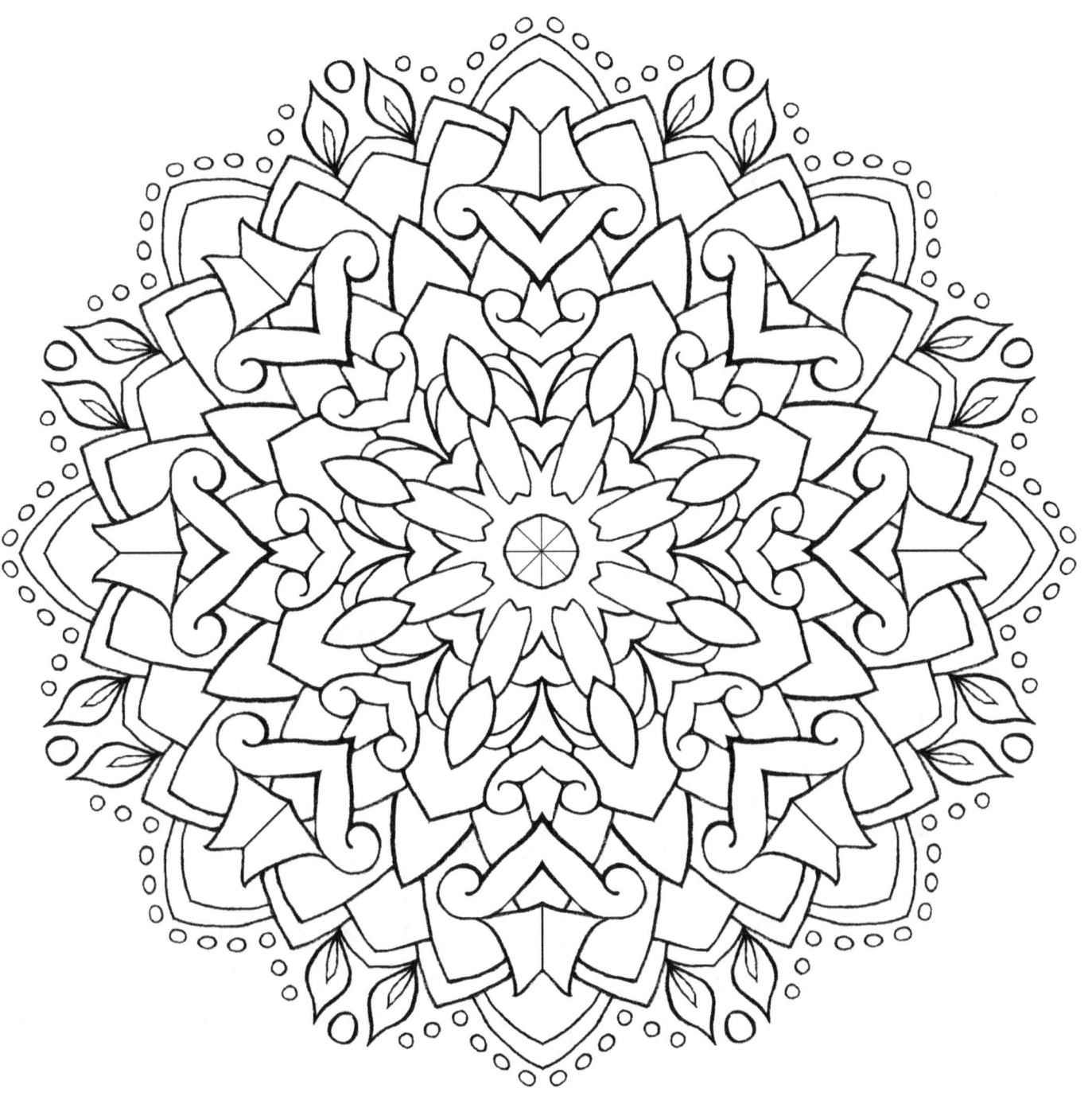

p.63   Colored by_____